# Angels

### THE

# Good
# BAD
# &
# UGLY

## TONY EVANS

ISBN 1-930893-01-9

**All material is taken from the teaching ministry of Dr. Tony Evans.**

You can contact The Urban Alternative by phone 1-800-800-3222 or by
e-mail: info@tonyevans.org or by visiting TonyEvans.org.

# CONTENTS

Dr. Evans' series of twelve messages titled Angels: Good Bad and Ugly is available on CD and MP3 download. For ordering information, contact The Urban Alternative at 1-800-800-3222 or by visiting TonyEvans.org.

# THE URBAN ALTERNATIVE

Dr. Tony Evans and The Urban Alternative (TUA) **equips, empowers,** and **unites** Christians to **impact** individuals, families, churches, and communities to restore hope and transform lives.

We believe the core cause of the problems we face in our personal lives, homes, churches, and societies is a spiritual one; therefore, the only way to address them is spiritually. We've tried a political, a social, an economic, and even a religious agenda. It's time for a Kingdom Agenda—God's visible and comprehensive rule over every area of life because when we function as we were designed, there is a divine power that changes everything. It renews and restores as the life of Christ is made manifest within our own. As we align ourselves under Him, there is an alignment that happens from deep within—where He brings about full restoration. It is an atmosphere that revives and makes whole.

As it impacts us, it impacts others—transforming every sphere of life in which we live. When each biblical sphere of life functions in accordance with God's Word, the outcomes are evangelism, discipleship, and community impact. As we learn how to govern ourselves under God, we then transform the institutions of family, church, and society from a biblically based kingdom perspective. Through Him, we are touching heaven and changing earth.

To achieve our goal, we use a variety of strategies, methods, and resources for reaching and equipping as many people as possible.

## BROADCAST MEDIA

Hundreds of thousands of individuals experience *The Alternative with Dr. Tony Evans* through the daily radio broadcast playing on more than **850 radio outlets** and in more than **130 countries.** The broadcast can also be seen on several television networks and is viewable online at TonyEvans.org.

## LEADERSHIP TRAINING

*The Kingdom Agenda Pastors (KAP)* provides a *viable network* for *like-minded pastors* who embrace the Kingdom Agenda philosophy. Pastors have the opportunity to go deeper with Dr. Tony Evans as they are given greater biblical knowledge, practical applications, and resources to impact individuals, families, churches, and communities. KAP welcomes senior and associate pastors of all churches.

*The Kingdom Agenda Pastors' Summit* progressively develops church leaders to meet the needs of the 21st century while maintaining the gospel message and the strategic position of the church. The Summit introduces *intensive seminars, workshops,* and *resources,* addressing issues affecting the community, family, leadership, organizational health, and more.

*Pastors' Wives Ministry,* founded by Dr. Lois Evans, provides *counsel, encouragement,* and *spiritual resources* for pastors' wives as they serve with their husbands in the ministry. A primary focus of the ministry is the KAP Summit that offers senior pastors' wives a safe place to *reflect, renew,* and *relax* along with training in personal development, spiritual growth, and care for their emotional and physical well-being.

## COMMUNITY IMPACT

*National Church Adopt-A-School Initiative (NCAASI)* prepares churches across the country to impact communities by using *public schools as the primary vehicle for effecting positive social change* in urban youth and families. Leaders of churches, school districts, faith-based organizations, and other nonprofit organizations are equipped with the knowledge and tools to *forge partnerships* and build *strong social service delivery systems.*

This training is based on the comprehensive church-based community impact strategy conducted by Oak Cliff Bible Fellowship. It addresses such areas as economic development, education, housing, health revitalization, family renewal, and racial reconciliation. We also assist churches in tailoring the model to meet the specific needs of their communities while simultaneously addressing the spiritual and moral frame of reference.

## RESOURCE DEVELOPMENT

We are fostering lifelong learning partnerships with the people we serve by providing a variety of published materials. We offer booklets, Bible studies, books, CDs, and DVDs to strengthen people in their walk with God and ministry to others.

* * *

For more information and a complimentary copy of Dr. Evans' devotional newsletter, call (800) 800-3222 or write TUA at P.O Box 4000, Dallas TX 75208, or log on to TonyEvans.org.

# INTRODUCTION

You may not realize it, but there are angels all around you. No, I'm not talking about spiritual beings created by God for His purposes. They're all around you, too, but I'm talking about the angels of popular culture.

If you have stepped outside your home for any length of time—and even if you haven't—I'm sure you know by now the angels are the "in" thing. Television is making lots of money off of angel programming. In these programs, angels interact with human beings in order to help them to straighten out their lives and solve their problems. Hollywood frequently offers us its version of angels, though Tinseltown's portrayals are less than accurate. You can buy angel pins to wear on your clothes. You can buy angel calendars to put on your desk at work. You can buy angels to put on top of your Christmas tree. Then there are magazines, books, greeting cards, costumes, paintings, coffee mugs, and T-shirts specifically designed with the angels' fan club in mind.

Angels are probably decorating a friend's house, a relative's home, maybe even your own home. And that's okay—they're kinda cute.

However, as Christians we need to be careful that we don't replace our worship of God with our worship of His angels. These spiritual creatures were not created to be worshiped; they were created to worship God and to assist the saints.

In fact, because the world is so intrigued by angels, God has given us a wonderful opportunity to start conversations with non-Christians about spiritual things. But before we can take advantage of the situation, we have to know what God says about angels. I believe you will be blessed as we begin a journey through the pages of God's Word to see what God has revealed to us about these heavenly beings that He has created.

This study is divided into three sections. In the first one, we look at the holy angels, where they come from, what their job is, how they operate, and how we can position ourselves to allow them to work on our behalf.

Then we'll turn to the subject of fallen angels, or demons. It is important to realize that demons are real and are very involved what is happening in our world today. Demons are another favorite topic for television shows and movies, so we need to be prepared to confront the myths with the truth found in Scripture. The Bible has warnings for us about the demonic domination, demonic teaching, and the whole program of Satan's full-time staff.
Finally we will deal with the chief of the fallen angels. You may know him as Lucifer, Satan, the devil, the serpent of old, the deceiver, the accuser, or one of his other names. We will look at his rebellion and fall, his character and strategies on his ultimate defeat.

As you work through these lessons, it is my prayer that you would begin to become more aware of what's going on around you. I don't believe God wants us to actively hunt for angels that are at work around us. However, when we are more sensitive to angelic activity, we won't be able to stop ourselves from recognizing God's hand in our lives and then returning to Him in praise and thanksgiving.

_Tony Evans_

# LESSON 1

## THE EXISTENCE OF ANGELS

*Angels are in...*vogue today. If you don't believe it, look around—there are angel clubs, angel stores, angel collectables, and all kinds of movies and TV programs about them. From "Highway to Heaven" to "Touched by an Angel" reruns, today's world is attempting to show the spiritual, supernatural force that affects people's lives.

> Because without the Word of God, we can't understand spiritual things.

Unfortunately, however, most of these attempts at explaining the spiritual realm of God's creation have fallen short...because without the Word of God, we can't understand spiritual things. The Bible says that we, as believers in Jesus Christ, are seated in heavenly places. And since there is so much activity occurring up there, where we really live, we need to be acquainted with what's going on.

Let's begin with the most obvious question one has when considering the subject of angels: What are they? Or, rather, who are they?

# 1. ANGELS ARE CREATED BEINGS

The first chapter of Colossians introduces us to the creation of angels. In verse 16, Paul says "For by Him [Christ] all things were created, both in the heavens and on earth, visible and invisible, whether thrones or dominions or rulers or authorities—all things have been created by Him and for Him." So there are two worlds, one that we can see (the invisible) and one that we can't see. Both were created by the same Person, Jesus Christ, in heaven and earth.

Just as there are earthly thrones, dominions, rulers, and authorities, there are also heavenly thrones, dominions, rulers and authorities. This spiritual, or Angelic, realm is more than a little mysterious, and sometimes we tend to get excited about it. Keep in mind, however, that the angels were not created as an order in themselves, but they were created for God's divine purpose.

For our struggle is not against flesh and blood, but against the ruler, against the powers, against the world forces of this darkness, against the spiritual forces of all wickedness in the heavenly places. Ephesians 6:12

Job 38 gives us some insight into the creation of angels:

*"Where were you when I laid the foundation of the earth? Tell Me, if you have understanding, who sets its measurements, since you know? Or who stretched the line on it? On what were its bases sunk? Or who laid its cornerstone, when the morning stars sang together, and all the sons of God shouted for joy?"*

*Job 38:4-7*

Think about the media has betrayed angels, some television to magazines to merchandise in the stores.  What is the danger in focusing too much attention on angels?  Read Colossians 2:18, then record your answers.

_____

_____

_____

_____

_____

_____

_____

In Job 38:7, the angels are referred to as morning stars.  Notice what they are doing.  Based on this verse, what kind of relationship do the angels have with their Creator?

_____

_____

_____

_____

_____

_____

# 2. ANGELS ARE SPIRITUAL BEINGS

Because angels belong to an invisible realm, we recognize that they are spiritual beings.  Hebrews 1:14 says, "Are they [angels] not all ministering spirits, sent out to render service for the sake of those who will inherit salvation?"

Angels are spirits, so we are not to look for them in simply physical forms. We are not supposed to be able to see them or touch them, because they are not flesh and blood. They are immaterial beings.

What the media has picked up on (although many times incorrectly) is that, though they are immaterial, non-physical beings, angels can and occasionally do become visible beings in order to carry out specific, sovereignly-directed supernatural activity on the earth.

**Read Hebrews 13:2. What should we keep in mind when showing hospitality to strangers? Both Abraham and Lot showed hospitality to strangers, according to the book of Genesis. Read chapters 18 and 19, and note what assignments the angels were carrying out.**

_____

_____

_____

_____

_____

_____

# 3. ANGELS ARE PERSONAL BEINGS

Not only were angels created to be spiritual beings, but they are also personal beings.  Personhood requires three parts: the emotions, intellect, and will.  Because angels meet these requirements, they are considered personal beings.

First of all, we know that angels have to have emotions because they like to party.  Luke 15:10 records Jesus as saying, "In the same way, I tell you, there is joy in the presence of the angels of God over one sinner who repents." In other words, these heavenly beings get together and have a good time whenever one of us gets saved!

Second, angels have intellect because they want to understand what redemption is all about.  First Peter 1:12 says,

*"It was revealed to them that they were not serv-ing themselves, but you, in these things which now have been announced to you through those who preached the gospel to you by the Holy Spirit sent from heaven-things into which angels long to look."*

> Angels are spirits, so we are not to look for them in simply physical frames.

Angels cannot fully comprehend redemption because Got never extended it to them. When Satan and his demons fell, their fate was sealed. Their fall also explains the will of angels, because they did have a choice to obey God or follow Satan.

**If angels, who cannot fully comprehend redemption, rejoice at the salvation of new believers, how much more should you rejoice over new brothers and sisters in Christ?**

_____
_____
_____
_____
_____
_____
_____

# 4. ANGELS ARE AN INNUMERABLE HOST OF BEINGS

Daniel 7:10 references a time when "thousands upon thousands" are attending God and "myriads upon myriads are standing before Him." A myriad is an indef-initely large number, so try thinking of it as 100 billion angels attending God at one time. And though angels do not procreate (Matthew 22:30), they do not die either. So whenever you worship, you are never worshiping alone. There is never one second of one day of one month of one year of one century of one millennium when God is not receiving 24 hour adoration.

**Do you realize that you are never alone when you're praising God? How will understanding this affect the way you worship?**

_____

_____

_____

_____

_____

_____

_____

There is never one second of one day of one month of one year of one century of one millennium when God is not receiving 24-hour adoration.

## 5. ANGELS ARE GLORIOUS BEINGS

Not only are the angels created beings, spiritual beings, personal beings, and an innumerable host of beings, but they are glorious beings. They are awesome creatures. Read Daniel 10:5-6 and note Daniel's description of this angelic stranger:

_"I lifted my eyes and looked, and behold, there was a certain man dressed in linen, whose waist was girded with a belt of pure gold of Uphaz. His body was like the beryl, his face had the appearance of lightning, his eyes were like flaming torches, his arms and feet like the gleam of polished bronze, and the sound of his words like the sound of a tumult."_

**Look up Acts 12:3-7 and read the account of Peter's escape from prison. But based on this description of an angel, can you see why Job (in Job 38:7) might have referred to angels as morning stars?**

_____

_____

_____

_____

_____

_____

_____

# 6. ANGELS ARE FUNCTIONAL BEINGS

Perhaps even more important to us than who angels are is what they do. First, they praise God. Their praise and worship is one of their primary tasks. Second, they execute the program of God. Angels are God's staff of employees, for He has chosen to use angels to accomplish His will in situations of life.

> *"The LORD has established his throne in the heavens; and His sovereignty rules over all. Bless the LORD, you His angels, mighty in strength, who perform His word, obeying the voice of His word! Bless the LORD, all you His hosts, you who serve Him, doing His will."*
>
> *Psalm 103:19-21*

**Angels are functional beings, and we see this again in Hebrews 1:14, where they are referred to as "ministering spirits."**

_____

_____

_____

_____

_____

_____

_____

_____

**Are they available to the general public?  Give the reason for your answer.**

_____

_____

_____

_____

_____

_____

**Read Hebrews 1:14 again. To whom do these angels minister? Give the reason for your answer.**

_____

_____

_____

_____

_____

_____

# 7. ANGELS ARE POWERFUL BEINGS

When God gets angry, His angels go to work. Psalm 18 offers a closer look at how God uses His angels for His service:

> "Then the earth shook and quaked; and the foundations of the mountains were trembling and were shaken, because He was angry.  Smoke went up out of His nostrils, and fire from His mouth

*devoured; coals were kindled by it. He bowed the heavens also, and came down with thick darkness under His feet. He rode upon a cherub and flew; and He sped upon the wings of the wind."*

*Psalm 18:7-10*

God was working through His natural catastrophe, and He was doing it by riding upon one of His cherubim. *His ride was connected with the "wings of the wind" that brought about this meteorological or if natural trembling on the earth.* Keep reading in verses 11-15:

*"He made darkness His hiding place, His canopy around Him, darkness of waters, thick clouds of the skies. From the brightness before Him passed His thick clouds, hailstones, and coals of fire. The LORD also thundered in the heavens, and the Most High uttered His voice, hailstones and coals of fire. He sent out His arrows, and scattered them, and lightning flashes in abundance, and routed them. Then the channels of water appeared, and the foundations of the world were laid bare. At Your rebuke, O LORD, at the blast of the breath of Your nostrils."*

In other words, when God moves in history, He often does so through His angels. That's why the whole book of Revelation is a book about angels. From chapter 1 through the end of the book, we see how angel after angel functions under God's rule.

When Jesus Christ returns to this earth, He will return with His mighty angels (2 Thessalonians 1:7). These creatures were not created just to fly around and look pretty, but they have been given awesome strength by our Creator. Do you remember who rolled the stone away from Jesus' tomb? When the women got there, the stone had been removed. Two angelic strangers were standing nearby (see Luke 24:2-4). Angels have been given incredible power to do God's work.

> Jesus has called
> His angels to minis-
> ter to us, but we're
> called to worship
> Him and Him alone.

Angels are intriguing, aren't they? So what should our response be to them? Shouldn't we go looking for them? No! Jesus has called His angels to minister to us, but we're called to worship Him and Him alone. Instead of getting excited over finding out the name of your angel, get excited over the name of Jesus Christ. He has a more excellent name.

**Though we have already seen the cherub's part in Psalm 18, what do you learn from verses 7-15 about God and His power?**

_____

_____

_____

_____

_____

_____

**Read Revelation 7:1; 8:12; 16:8. What kind of control do these angels have over nature?**

_____

_____

_____

_____

_____

_____

# LESSON 2

## THE MINISTRY OF ANGELS

*Behind that...* which is visible lies another world *that is invisible, and our relationship to the invisible world will determine our relationship to the visible world. There is a conflict raging in the heavenlies, and we are in the middle of it. It is a spiritual conflict that does not involve people. And if Satan can get us to fight each other rather than fighting spiritually, then he has us fighting on his territory, and according to his rules.*

> And He said to him, "Truly, truly, I say to you, you shall see the heavens opened, and the angels of God ascending and descending on the Son of Man." John 1:51

If that thought frightens you, there's good news. God has provided angelic help as we fight and wage this spiritual battle. We are not alone. Not only do we have God on our side, but we have the staff of God. Angels are the ones God has chosen to execute His historical plan. Could He do it without angels? Absolutely. But He has chosen to work through His creatures in order to accomplish His program.

As we look at the ministry of angels, ask God to open your mind to understand His Word. Pray that you would be more sensitive to these ministering spirits who serve you according to the will of the Creator.

Also remember that, even though we want to understand how angels work in our lives and in the lives of other believers, all our praise and gratitude should always be pointed to Jesus Christ. We need to thank Him for always providing us with what we need.

# 1. NATHANAEL SAW ANGELS AT WORK

Nathanael was resting under a fig tree. He was taking it easy, engaged in thought, with no idea of what was about to happen. Though he didn't know it at the time, he was in for a surprise—he was about to meet the Son of God.

> *"The next day He purposed to go forth into Galilee, and He found Philip. And Jesus said to him, "Follow Me." Now Philip was from Bethsaida, of the city of Andrew and Peter. Philip found Nathanael and said to him, "We have found Him of whom Moses in the Law and also the Prophets wrote, Jesus of Nazareth, the son of Joseph." And Nathanael said to him, "Can any good thing come out of Nazareth?" Philip said to him, "Come and see." Jesus saw Nathanael coming to Him, and said of him, "Behold, an Israelite indeed, in whom is no guile!" Nathanael said to Him, "How do You know me?" Jesus answered and said to him, "Before Philip called you, when you were under the fig tree, I saw you." Nathanael answered Him, "Rabbi, You are the Son of God; You are the King of Israel." Jesus answered and said to him, "Because I said to you that I saw you under the fig tree, do you believe? You shall see greater things than these." And He said to him, "Truly, truly, I say to you, you shall see the heavens opened, and the angels of God ascending and descending on the Son of Man."*
>
> *John 1:43:-51*

Nathanael recognized Jesus as the Son of God, the King of Israel. And because of that affirmation, Jesus promised him that he would get to see heavenly activity. He would see angels of God ascending and descending on Jesus.

Where did Nathanael's affirmation come from? What was it that immediately convinced him that Jesus was not just an ordinary man or a good guesser?

Obviously, the fact that Jesus knew he had been under the fig tree gave him a clue that something was up. But there may have been another hint. Jesus may have revealed to Nathanael His omniscience when He said, "Behold, an Israelite indeed, in whom is no guile!" (v. 47)

> Though Nathanael didn't know it at the time he was in for a surprise. He was about to meet the Son of God.

**If you have dictionary, look up the definition of the word guile. What examples from the Old Testament might you give for someone who had guile?**

_____

_____

_____

_____

_____

_____

_____

## 2. JACOB SAW ANGELS AT WORK

You may have recalled Jacob as one who had guile. From craftily obtaining his brother's birthright to deceiving both his father and father-in law, Jacob was a man continually haunted by his actions.

However, God loved Jacob and had a plan to capture his attention.

> *"Then Jacob departed from Beersheba and went toward Haran. He came to a certain place and spent the night there, because the sun had set; and he took one of the stones of the place and put it under his head, and lay down in that place. He had a dream, and behold, a ladder was set on the earth with its top reaching to heaven; and behold, the angels of God were ascending and descending on it."*
>
> *Genesis 28:10-12*

What did Jacob see while he was resting and relaxing? He saw angels ascending and descending on a heavenly staircase! God, in an act of sovereign grace, allowed him to get a view of heaven and let him know that he was going to be with Him.

## 3. HOW DO ANGELS WORK?

In all probability, Nathanael wasn't thinking about Jacob's ladder and those angels when Philip showed up. If so, he would have been meditating on Jacob's guile. For Jesus to say that Nathanael had no guile was to say, "I know where you were, and I know what you were thinking. I am God."

Now, let's take a closer look at the ladder Jacob saw in Genesis 28. The ladder was on earth, but its top reached to heaven. If we are going to be spiritually successful on earth, we must have access to heaven. Why? Because, everything that happens on earth is precipitated by something that has preceded it in heaven.

Four important principles can be found in Jacob's dream about this ladder:

**A.** *With the ladder came God's* **PROMISES** (Genesis 28:13-14). During Jacob's dream, God spoke about a promise that He would fulfill. He promised to give the land to Jacob's descendants; spread out his descendants and make them like the dust of the earth; bless the descendants in the family; be with him; keep him wherever he went; and bring him back to the land.

One of the biggest tragedies among Christians today is that many of us do not know the promises that God has made, based on His own name and His own character, that He is committed to fulfilling. And Satan wants to keep us ignorant because we cannot claim what we do not know. A working knowledge of the Word of God is critical to the experience of the ladder—our access to heaven.

**B.** *With the ladder came God's* **PRESENCE** (Genesis 28:15). A lot of times, we don't recognize the presence of God. Jacob was not spiritually sensitive until after this event. Nathanael had the wisdom to acknowledge Jesus as the Son of God.

**C**. *With the ladder came God's* **PROTECTION** (Genesis 28:15). God said to Jacob, "I will keep you." When heaven is properly linked to earth this way, we can relax—because our lives can then be linked to heaven, and nothing can happen to us outside of God's will.

If we are going to be spiritually successful on earth, we must have access to heaven.

Speaking of protection, why don't you pause for a minute and read 2 Kings 6:8-18? You'll be greatly encouraged.

> "Now the king of Aram was warring against Israel…he sent horses and chariots and a great army there, and they came by night and surrounded the city. Now when the attendant of the man of God had risen early and gone out, behold, an army with horses and chariots was circling the city. And his servant said to him, 'Alas, my master! What shall we do?' So he answered. 'Do not fear, for those who are with us are more than those who are with them.' Then Elisha prayed and said, 'O LORD, I pray, open his eyes that he may see.' And the LORD opened the servant's eyes, and he saw; and behold, the mountain was full of horses and chariots of fire all around Elisha. And when they came down to him, Elisha prayed to the LORD and said, 'Strike this people with blindness, I pray.' So He struck them with blindness according to the word of Elisha."
>
> *2 Kings 6:8, 14-18*

One of the biggest tragedies among Christians today is that many of us do not know the promises that God has made and is committed to fulfilling.

Elisha was being surrounded by angels with chariots of fire. Whenever you see chariots of fire, you can know you have angelic protection. He was surrounded by angelic protection, and his servant couldn't even see it.

You cannot pray for what you cannot see through the eyes of faith, but Elisha could see. The attendant couldn't pray because he couldn't see.

If you are spiritually blind, you don't know what you have access to. He couldn't see spiritually and as a result, couldn't pray properly.

Many of us won't call on God for what He is willing to do—and often waiting to do—because we don't see that He's able to do it. We don't see this ladder that connects between heaven and earth. And so what do we do? We quit, give up, run, or say, "I can't."

> You cannot pray for what you cannot see through the eyes of faith.

We hear what the devil says, but we don't hear what God says. We act on his will rather than on God's will. Because Elisha saw, he knew that he could be confident even in a dangerous situation.

**D**. *With the ladder came God's* **PROVISION** (Genesis 28:15). God promised Jacob that He would provide for him. Another example of His provision can be found in 1 Kings. Elijah, who was the forerunner of Elisha was having some problems with Jezebel. In fact, she had ordered his death.

> *"Now Ahab told Jezebel all that Elijah had done, and how he had killed all the prophets with the sword. Then Jezebel sent a messenger to Elijah saying, "So may the gods do to me and even more, if I do not make your life as the life of one of them by tomorrow about this time. And he was afraid and arose and ran for his life and came to Beersheba, which belonged to Judah, and left his servant there."*
>
> *1 Kings 19:1-3*

When you're at your worst, not only can God take care of you—and not only can He take care of you well—but He can keep you going for the length of time until He's ready to show you His next plan for your life. He can cover you from cover to cover, pillar to post, beginning to end. And He does it through His angels.

Look at one more example. Matthew 4:11 says, "Then the devil left Him [Christ]; and behold, angels came and began to minister to Him." Whenever you face a difficult circumstance, you need to do something spiritual. In times of difficulty, Elijah was honest with God, Elisha prayed, and Jesus spoke the Word of God. Though they all encountered difficulties, they were able to overcome those problems because they were spiritually attuned.

> Many of us won't call on God for what He is willing to do—and often waiting to do—because we don't see that He's able to do it.

**On a separate sheet of paper, make a list of as many of God's promises as you can think of.**

**When you finish, write out a prayer thanking Him for two or three of those promises that mean the most to you right now.**

_____

_____

_____

_____

_____

_____

_____

_____

_____

_____

Have you missed God's presence in your life when things have gotten tough? How will this study of angels help you to be sensitive to the help available in this spiritual realm?

_____

_____

_____

_____

_____

_____

What are some common excuses you have used or have heard others use in pulling back from God's will? How will you respond in the light of these passages? Why?

_____

_____

_____

_____

_____

_____

What steps will you take to prepare yourself to be spiritually attuned? Read the accounts of Jesus' temptation in Matthew 4 or Luke 4. What Scriptures could you use in a trial or temptation?

_____

_____

_____

_____

_____

_____

If heaven is way out there somewhere and earth is way down here, then you need to look to Jesus, who can bridge that gap for you.

## 4. WE CAN SEE ANGELS AT WORK

Jacob saw the ladder and soon began to realize all that God was offering. Elijah and Elisha both turned to Him and received what He had to offer. Nathanael recognized Jesus as the Son of God, and Jesus promised the same for him. However, when Jesus said in John 1:51 that "you shall see," He was not just referring to Nathanael.

In the Greek, the word "you" is plural. So this promise is not only to Nathanael, but to all followers of Jesus Christ (this includes you if you have believed in Him).

**How do you need to see heaven and earth come together in your life? If heaven is way out there somewhere and earth is way down here, then you need to look to Jesus, who can bridge that gap for you. The ministry of angels always points back to the Creator—Jesus Christ.**

_____

_____

_____

_____

_____

_____

_____

# NOTES

# THE OPERATION
# OF ANGELS

*Angels can be...* very involved in our lives, but
*they always operate by authority. God is not a God of confusion (1 Corinthians*
*14:33), so whenever He operates or puts His angels to work on our behalf,*
*that work is always done in an orderly fashion.*

> Satan, however, desires to bring about
> confusion, disruption, and disharmony.

He wants to cause chaos, conflict, and disunity. The reason he wants believers battling it out with each other is because he wants to hinder our prayers (see 1 Peter 3:7). Because confusion and chaos would contradict the nature of God, He will not work in this type of environment.

## 1. ANGELS ARE ORGANIZED BY AUTHORITY

The organizational structure of the angelic realm was established by Jesus Christ (Colossians 1:16). Not only did Christ create earthly thrones, dominions, rulers, and authorities, but He also made invisible thrones, dominions, rulers, and authorities. There is a structured, organized spiritual regime that is parallel to the earthly structure. Both involve an ordered process. So behind every earthly king is an angel or demon who can pull the strings.

A chain of command exists in the spiritual realm just as it does in the physical realm. This is even true of Satan's camp, because the devil always attempts to mimic God.

Before Satan fell, he was Lucifer the archangel, the anointed cherub. In other words, he was number one. He was the first of the angelic realm. God had placed him in the position of ruler over the angelic realm. So there was a chain of command in the way God structured the universe to be run by angels.

Angels can be classified into three categories, and each category is different in function.

The first group mentioned in the Bible is the cherubim, who serve as a type of royal guard. Cherubim were placed in front of the Garden of Eden to keep Adam and Eve from returning to the garden or eating again from the Tree of Life.

Seraphim, best described in Isaiah 6, are particularly concerned with the holiness of God, These beings are described by Isaiah as "each having six wings; with two he covered his face, and with two he covered his feet, and with two he flew" (Isaiah 6:2).

The third class of angels—the four living creatures—are found in the book of Revelation. These creatures never cease to worship their Creator.

God is not a God of confusion but of peace as in all the churches of the saints. 1 Corinthians 14:33

"And before the throne there was, something like a sea of glass, like crystal; and in the center and around the throne, four living creatures full of eyes in front and behind. The first creature was like a lion, and the second creature like a *calf, and the third creature had a face like that of a man, and the fourth creature was like a flying eagle. And the four living creatures, each one of them having six wings, are full of eyes around and within; and day and night they do not cease to say, "Holy, Holy, Holy, is the Lord God, the Almighty, who was and who is and who is to come."*

*Revelation 4:6-8*

Angels can be classified into three categories, and each category is different in function.

**By what authority is the spiritual realm organized?**

_____

_____

_____

_____

_____

_____

_____

**Read Genesis 3:22-24, 2 Samuel 22:11, and Ezekiel 10:9-16. What are the functions of the cherubim? Seraphim? Four living creatures?**

_____

_____

_____

_____

_____

_____

_____

## 2. ANGELS UNDERSTAND THE IMPORTANCE OF AUTHORITY

Michael the archangel understood the importance of authority. When conflict erupted between Michael and Satan, he stood his ground by invoking the authority of the Lord. "But Michael the archangel, when he disputed with the devil and argued about the body of Moses, did not dare pronounce against him a railing judgment, but said, 'The Lord rebuke you" (Jude 9).

The Roman centurion accurately applied the principle of authority in Matthew 8. Though, this particular account involved a human being and his understanding of Jesus' authority, the principle remains the same. The centurion was worried about his servant, who was paralyzed and suffering great pain.

Jesus agreed to heal the servant, but the centurion stopped Him saying,

> "Lord, I am not worthy for You to come under my roof, but just say the word, and my servant will be healed. For I too am a man under authority, with soldiers under me; and I say to this one, 'Go!' and he goes, and to another, 'Come!' and he comes, and to my slave, 'Do this!' and he does it."
>
> Matthew 8:8-9

Angels can be classified into three categories, and each category is different in function.

The principle of authority simply says that when one appeals to an authority over him to do something that one under him cannot do, then it is the responsibility of the one over him to act on behalf of the one under him.

**Look up the following passages and note what things Jesus has authority over: Matthew 2:6; 7:29; 28:18-20; Mark 1:27; Luke 5:24; John 5:22,27; 1 Peter 3:22.**

_____

_____

_____

_____

_____

_____

_____

# 3. ANGELS ARE LOYAL TO THEIR AUTHORITY

Because angels recognize the importance of authority, they remain loyal to it. Jesus pointed this out when He was accused of performing miracles in the devil's power.

> "And knowing their thoughts He said to them, any kingdom divided against itself is laid waste; and any city or house divided against itself shall not stand. And if Satan casts out Satan, he is divided against himself; how then shall his kingdom stand?"
>
> _Matthew 12:25-26_

The angels remain loyal to their authority. Why? Because the two kingdoms are tight, and the angels in both camps must be committed to one or the other. Angels don't straddle the spiritual fence, and there are no part-time angels.

If you're a part-time saint, don't expect to see much of God. Friendship with the world is hostility toward God (James 4:4). The only way you'll see God's authority operating in your life is by pledging total allegiance to His kingdom.

**How can our disloyalty affect our relationship with God? Read James 4:1-10 before answering.**

_____

_____

_____

_____

_____

_____

_____

## 4. ANGELS EXERCISE THEIR AUTHORITY IN HISTORY THROUGH PEOPLE

The principle of authority simply says that when one appeals to an authority over him to do something that one under him cannot do, then it is the responsibility of the one over him to act on behalf of the one under him.

One of the primary ways angels accomplish their work is through people. This is true of both good and bad angels. Satan's angels especially like to use people who will twist the teaching of God's Word.

_"But the Spirit explicitly says that in later times some will fall away from the faith, paying attention to deceitful spirits and doctrines of demons, by means of the hypocrisy of liars seared in their own conscience as with a branding iron, men who forbid marriage and advocate abstaining from foods which God has created to be gratefully shared in by those who believe and know the truth."_

_1 Timothy 4:1-3_

Notice who delivers this demonic teaching, men who lie! Satan's demons promote their agenda through the control of men. False teachers are dangerous, but the fact that they're out there just underscores our need to be spiritually attuned and to surround ourselves with others who are spiritually attuned as well. One of the gifts of the Spirit is discernment, and one thing that often must be discerned is whether a problem is being demonically promoted.

> If you're a part-time saint, don't expect to see much of God. Friendship with the world is hostility toward God.

The book of Daniel, which is full of angelic activity, also shows angels exercising their authority. Daniel received a visit from an angelic being described as having a face like the appearance of lightning, eyes like flaming torches, arms and feet like the gleam of polished bronze, and a voice like the sound of a tumult (Daniel 10:6).

The angel had come in response to Daniel's prayers (v. 12). Though he had been trying to get to Daniel, he had been prevented by another angel. "But the prince of the kingdom of Persia was withstanding me for twenty-one days; then behold, Michael, one of the chief princes, came to help me, for I had been left there with the kings of Persia" (v. 13).

Persia was an earthly kingdom, but it had behind it a demonic prince who was controlling events. That demonic prince was getting in the way of the angel who had been sent with the answer to Daniel's prayer.

When the angel was unable to break through to get the answer to Daniel, he invoked the principle of authority and called on Michael. He needed help from a higher authority, so he sought out the archangel.

If you're frustrated because your prayer seemingly hasn't been answered, just be patient. Whatever it is could be tied to an event outside of you, above you, and beyond you. Our responsibility is to keep praying and trust that His answer will come in His perfect timing. God is never late in answering our prayers.

**Read 2 Timothy 2:15 and John 17:17. What can you do to avoid being deceived by the "doctrines of demons?"**

_____

_____

_____

_____

_____

_____

_____

_____

_____

**Read Luke 11:5-10. What principle does this parable offer for your prayer life?**

_____

_____

_____

_____

_____

_____

_____

_____

_____

# 5. ANGELS ARE ACTIVATED BY AUTHORITY

The principle of authority also applies to the activation of angels. See how this principle is demonstrated in 1 Corinthians 11:3-5,10:

> *"But I want you to understand that Christ is the head of every man, and the man is the head of a woman, and God is the head of Christ. Every man who has something on his head while praying or prophesying disgraces his head. But every woman who has her head uncovered while praying or prophesying disgraces her head; for she is one and the same with her whose head is shaved. . . Therefore the woman ought to have a symbol of authority on her head, because of the angels."*

When the angel was unable to break through to get the answer to Daniel, he invoked the principle of authority and called on Michael. He needed help from a higher authority, so he sought out the archangel.

The angels are very involved in the activities of the saints. This passage deals specifically with church worship. In order for the angels to do what they're supposed to do, the people for whom they are doing it must be doing what they are supposed to be doing.

To put it another way, if you rebel against authority with the angels watching (in this case, the lack of covering because the woman was rebelling against the male head), you have rebuffed the angels. And you cannot expect angelic assistance when you are not operating under the principle of authority.

While this passage singles out women, the principle applies equally to men because men are under Christ. When men rebel against the authority of Christ, then that protective covering or angelic hedge has been removed.

**How do you respond to God-given authority in your life? If you were to require angelic assistance, what kind of response do you think you would receive?**

_____

_____

_____

_____

_____

_____

_____

## 6. ANGELS ARE UNDER GOD'S SOVEREIGN AUTHORITY

The reason we can win the battle is that the angels are under God's sovereign authority. Maybe you have begun to recognize angelic activity in your life. If so, you may feel like worshiping the angels. That's a danger you want to avoid. When John received the revelation from Jesus' angel, he was so overcome that he started to worship the angel. But the angel himself warned John to worship God instead (Revelation 22:9). So don't go angel hunting. Go God hunting.

If He gives you an angel, fine. Thank God for the angel, but remember that it's God who gets the glory. God never created an angel to get the glory that should go to Him who created the angel.

Maybe you're in a difficult situation right now. Maybe your prayers have not been answered. Maybe you're struggling as you try to understand why. You can rest in the knowledge of God's sovereignty. He has created angelic beings to minister to you. And though there's a conflict between good and evil in the spiritual realm, you will receive your answer in God's perfect timing. He will not let you suffer more than you can handle (1 Corinthians 10:13). He is sovereign even over the angels, and He is in control of your life's circumstances.

**Read Job 1:1-2:6. Note the limits God gave Satan when he wanted to cause Job to stumble. What comfort can you take from understanding God's sovereignty?**

_____

_____

_____

_____

_____

_____

_____

In order for the angels to do what they're supposed to do, the people for whom they are doing it must be doing what they are supposed to be doing.

# NOTES

# NOTES

# LESSON 4

## THE ACTIVATION OF ANGELS

# We wrestle... *"not against flesh and blood, but against the rulers, against the powers, against the world forces of this darkness, and against the spiritual forces of wickedness in the heavenly places" (Ephesians 6:12). That's why the church of Jesus Christ needs to understand how to activate angels.*

When you get a credit card in the mail, the first thing you have to do is activate it. Otherwise, you won't be able to use it. If you go to the gas station and swipe your card upside down, the card will not activate the gas pump. The pump must be activated correctly.

> So our authority comes from a right relationship with God.

This same principle applies to the spirit world. In order to activate angels, we must position ourselves so that God can allow His agents, the angels, to work on our behalf. This doesn't mean that we can force angels to do anything; they have no obligation to us. Angels only listen to their boss, and that boss is either Jesus Christ or the devil.

So our authority comes from a right relationship with God. If that relationship is in place, He is predisposed to designate angelic activity on our behalf.

# 1. WE ACTIVATE ANGELS THROUGH WORSHIPING GOD

When we are worshiping God, we have put the card in the right slot, the right way. On the other hand, we can deactivate angels by not worshiping.

Angels were created to worship God, and when we join them in doing what they do best, God activates them on our behalf.

Hebrews 12:22 says, "But you have come to Mount Zion and to the city of the living God, the heavenly Jerusalem, and to myriads of angels." Angels were created to worship God, and when we join them in doing what they do best, God activates them on our behalf.

**What does the word "worship" mean to you? What do you think it involves? What is the primary way you worship God?**

_____

_____

_____

_____

_____

_____

_____

_____

_____

## 2. WE WORSHIP THROUGH PRAISE

In Isaiah 6, the prophet was having a hard time because King Uzziah had died. Israel was finally flourishing under Uzziah's leadership, but now Uzziah was dead. Maybe some of your "Uzziahs" have died—things in life that you counted on, a job Uzziah, a health Uzziah, a circumstance Uzziah. Whatever it is, it's gone. And the hope you were placing in that thing or that set of circumstances is no longer available.

When your Uzziah dies, when your circumstances plummet, join the angels. That's what Isaiah did. The passage says, "In the year of King Uzziah's death, I saw the Lord sitting on a throne, lofty and exalted, with the train of His robe filling the temple. Seraphim stood above Him. . . . and one called out to another and said, 'Holy, Holy, Holy, is the Lord of hosts, the whole earth is full of His glory'" (v. 1-3).

The first fundamental area of worship that activates angels is praise. When Isaiah went to the temple on earth, he was transported to the temple in heaven. And at the temple in heaven, he saw the seraphim doing in heaven what he 'came to do on earth'—worship.

We join the angels whenever we worship because it's an ongoing, nonstop activity for them. Notice that there are four wings for worship and two for working. You should always spend more time in worship than working. That way, when you get to work, you have already spent enough time in His presence to know what He wants you to do.

King Uzziah had died, and Israel's circumstances were in a mess that year. That's why Isaiah went to the temple. But when he got there and saw what God was about, it changed how he viewed his earthly circumstances. Then something awesome happened in verse 4: "The foundations of the thresholds trembled at the voice of him who called out, while the temple was filling with

We join the angels whenever we worship because it's an ongoing, nonstop activity for them. When you're unclear of God's will, it's time to worship.

smoke." This was no little whispering worship. The place was shaking! The foundations were shaking! And the temple was filling with smoke!

Isaiah saw his God high and lifted up. And what was his reply? "Woe is me!" (v. 5). Whenever you see God in all His holiness, you get a new view of yourself, and it's not pretty.

The word woe means "undone" or "coming apart at the seams." Isaiah felt this way because he had a new perspective of himself after witnessing the holiness of God. And then what happened? The angels began to move.

When Isaiah went to worship, God gave an angel the responsibility of putting hot coals to his lips in order to clean up, or purify, his life.

By verse 8, Isaiah had a mission and knew what to do with his life. He had gone to the temple to worship the Lord and ended up in the company of angels.

When you're unclear of God's will, it's time to worship. When you reach a fork in the road and don't know which direction to take, it's time to worship. When you're utterly confused because your circumstances are falling apart, it's time to praise Him.

**Where is the first place you turn when life throws you a curve? How can worshiping God benefit you in an immediate, practical way?**

_____

_____

_____

_____

_____

_____

_____

**Read 2 Chronicles 20:1-23. When King Jehoshaphat was in trouble, how did he pray? What was the focus of his prayer?**

_____

_____

_____

_____

_____

_____

_____

# 3. WE WORSHIP THROUGH SACRIFICE

Sacrifice is another area of worship that activates angels. When we sacrifice, we take something of value to us and give it to God.

Throughout the Bible, God regularly calls His people to sacrifice before He blesses them, because sacrifice is an act of faith. Remember Abraham in Genesis 22? God told Abraham to sacrifice his only son, Isaac, as an act of faith.

So Abraham took his son, tied him to the altar, and prepared to take his life. When God saw that Abraham would not withhold even his son from Him, He stopped him from killing Isaac. A ram had been waiting in the thicket.

God will send His angels with the answer to your prayers when He knows you're willing to make the sacrifice. But Abraham's angel didn't show up until Abraham was about to come down to the point of absolute conformity to the expectation of God. That's when the angel pointed out the ram in the thicket.

God has the answers to our problems, and He has an angel ready to send the answers. But He wants to know if we're going to carry out our obedience all the way.

David offered another example of sacrifice in 1 Chronicles 21. David was overcome with pride as he decided to number his military men. This decision upset God because it meant David was shifting his faith from God to his human ability. God does not like pride because it reminds Him of Satan's fall.

Now, in order for David to get out of this mess, he had to build an altar. So he went to Oman and asked for a place to build it.

God will send His angels with the answer to your prayers when He knows you're willing to make the sacrifice.

And Ornan said to David,

> "Take it for yourself; and let my lord the king do what is good in his sight. See, I will give the oxen for burnt offerings and the threshing sledges for wood and the wheat for the grain offering; I will give it all." But King David said to Ornan, "No, but I will surely buy it for the full price; for I will not take what is yours for the Lord or offer a burnt offering which costs me nothing."
>
> 1 Chronicles 21:23-24

Remember that phrase: "God, I will not offer You something that costs me nothing." A lot of us want free worship. We want the blessings of God without any sacrifice on our part. But David understood the principle of sacrifice.

And in verse 27, it says, "And the Lord commanded the angel, and he put his sword back in its sheath." Because of David's sacrifice, judgment was withheld.

If you have sinned against God, and if you deserve judgment but desperately want grace, then you need to do what David did: sacrifice unto the Lord. Take something you value and give it up for the glory of God. You may need to give up your time, your money, or certain resources. We cannot rob God and win. Worship includes sacrifice.

If you have sinned against God, and if you deserve judgment but desperately want grace, then you need to do what David did: sacrifice unto the Lord.

**Are you "counting your soldiers" as David did? Is there an element of pride in your life that you need to release? Record it below, then go to God and confess it.**

_____

_____

_____

_____

_____

_____

_____

**Are you willing to give up something of value to you in order to get back from God something more valuable than that which you gave up?**

_____

_____

_____

_____

_____

_____

_____

# 4. WE WORSHIP THROUGH PRAYER

Zacharias was in the middle of his priestly service when he received an angelic visit (see Luke 1:8-11). And in Acts 12, because the church was praying, an angel appeared on the scene to break Peter out of prison (Acts 12:5-7, 11-12). In fact, the church was in shock that their prayer was answered (v. 15)!

It's a terrible thing to pray when we don't even believe what we're praying for. God is Sovereign, and He is the One who will make the ultimate decisions. But if you have a legitimate request and a legitimate need, then go to God in prayer and expect a legitimate answer.

Prayer is important to God. In Genesis 18, Abraham intervened for Lot and his family. Because Abraham talked to God, two angels delivered them from the destruction of the city.

Some of us desperately need to pray because we're in a lions' den situation. Maybe a husband, a wife, or a boss is roaring at you. Remember, Daniel was in a lions' den too.

When King Darius signed into law an injunction that would prohibit prayer, Daniel kept on praying—with his windows open (Daniel 6:10). Now prayer does not keep us from getting thrown into the lions' den. A lot of people think, "Because I pray, nothing should happen." No. Because you pray, you're not alone when something happens. There's a big difference.

So the king came along to check on Daniel. He wanted to know if the lions had eaten him.

> *"And when he had come near the den to Daniel, he cried out with a troubled voice. The king spoke and said to Daniel, "Daniel, servant of the living God, has your God, whom you constantly serve, been able to deliver you from the lions?" Then Daniel spoke to the king, "O king, live forever! My God sent His angel and shut the lions' mouths, and they have not harmed me, inasmuch as I was found innocent before Him; and also toward you, O king, I have commit-ted no crime."*
>
> *Daniel 6:20-22*

How did those lions lose their appetite? Angelic intervention. Daniel could have tried all he wanted to close the lions' mouths, but it wouldn't have worked. Many Christians are trying to close the mouths of the lions who are threatening to devour them, and it isn't working. God's angels can do a better job than we can. But before they can do a better job than we can, we have to get God's attention. And the way to get God's attention is through passionate prayer.

Even Jesus understood this, because He had to function as a man. "And He withdrew from them about a stone's throw, and He knelt down and began to pray saying, 'Father, if Thou art willing, remove this cup from Me; yet not My will, but Thine be done'" (Luke 22:41-42).

That's how we should pray.

When Jesus Christ was facing something He didn't like and didn't want to face, He asked the Father to remove it. But then, after He asked the Father to remove it, He said "Not My will, but Thine be done." In other words, here's what I want. But what I want more than what I want, is what You want for me.

# LESSON 4

It's a terrible thing to pray when we don't even believe what we're praying for.

But suppose His will doesn't match our request? Then the angels step in. Luke 22:43 says, "Now an angel from heaven appeared to Him, strengthening Him." God will always do one of two things: He will either give you what you asked for, or He will give you angelic strength to deal with what He wants.

**What consequence did Daniel face for ignoring the king's injunction? How did God extend angelic assistance to him?**

_____

_____

_____

_____

_____

_____

## 5. WE WORSHIP THROUGH SUBMISSION

Angels always operate under authority, and submission means coming underneath the proper authority. So the next aspect of worship is submission to God. We will never receive angelic help from God if we're bucking His legitimate authority. If you're a child bucking the authority of your parents, forget angelic assistance. If you're a wife bucking the authority of your husband, forget angelic assistance. If you're a husband bucking the authority of Christ, forget angelic assistance.

Because angels operate under authority, they know when we are or are not operating under authority. In Acts 19:15, some Jewish exorcists were attempting to cast out demons. The evil spirit said, "I recognize Jesus, and I know about Paul, but who are you?" Then the demons attacked the exorcists. Even these fallen angels realized the importance of authority, and the Jewish exorcists had none.

The activation of angels means positioning ourselves so that God can put angels in motion on our behalf. Just remember that only God puts the angels in motion.

So, again, don't worship angels. Don't go angel hunting. Angels are fellow servants. Worship God. It is in worship that angelic activity is dispensed to God's people.

**Have you submitted to the proper authority in your life? Ask God to show you if and why angelic assistance has been withheld.**

_____

_____

_____

_____

_____

_____

_____

A lot of people think nothing should happen. No, because you pray, you're not alone when something happens.

# NOTES

# NOTES

# THE EXISTENCE
# OF DEMONS

*Everything visible...* and physical has an invisible and spiritual cause. But because most people don't understand this, they live their visible and physical lives without properly relating to the invisible spiritual world.

In our study, we have seen that angels are God's agents. They are His staff. He has decided to administer His program angelically by allowing angels to assist His people in the kingdom program. However, there is another group of angels working through mankind in order to achieve the agenda of hell. These angels are the fallen angels, or demons.

> However, there is another group of angels working though mankind in order to achieve the agenda of hell.

These demons are outside forces that wreak havoc in this visible, physical world, making it necessary for believers to understand how they work so that we can be prepared to win this spiritual battle.

# 1. THE ORIGIN OF DEMONS

Sometimes people struggle with the origin of Satan and his demons. It's hard to understand how a good and loving God could create such evil. The truth is, He didn't.

When God created the angelic host, He created them in perfection. They were perfect. Even Satan, the head of the demons, was created in beauty and was a wonder to behold (Ezekiel 28:12). All of God's angels were magnificently created.

Satan was not created as an evil angel. He chose to rebel against God. When pride welled up in his heart, he walked away. He did not want to accept God as the only sovereign one. Because of his rebellion, God removed him from heaven and cast him down to earth. But he didn't go alone. "And his [Satan's] tail swept away a third of the stars of heaven, and threw them to the earth" (Revelation 12:4).

Satan is called "the prince of the power of the air" (Ephesians 2:2), meaning that he controls the demonic regime, or kingdom, that influences certain events on earth. He deceives the whole world (Revelation 12:9) through his demons, who assist his program of opposition to God and His people.

Although God created all the angels as perfect creatures, demons chose to follow Satan in his rebellion against God. These demons now dwell in Satan's camp and are loyal only to him.

One reason the people did not want to believe that Jesus Christ was casting out demons by the power of God was because they would then have to acknowledge that God was with Him.

Jesus pointed out this loyalty to the multitudes after He was accused of casting out demons by the devil's power (see Matthew 12:22-30).

One reason the people did not want to believe that Jesus Christ was casting out demons by the power of God was because they would then have to acknowledge that God was with Him. If God was with Him, that meant He was who He claimed to be—the Son of God. So, in order to reject Him as the Son of God, they rejected the power He demonstrated.

Jesus pointed out that Beelzebul runs a kingdom in which there is no division. Satan's demonic regime is successful and powerful in disrupting our lives because of its unity. Demons are loyal and committed to their leader. And just as the power of hell is seen in the unity of the unrighteous empire of hell, the power of God cannot be seen unless there is a unified impact from the powers of heaven. This is precisely why one of Satan's main goals is to divide people—because he knows a divided kingdom cannot stand.

"And another sign appeared in heaven: and behold, a great red dragon having seven heads and ten horns, and on his heads were seven diadems. And his tail swept away a third of the stars of heaven, and threw them to the earth." Revelation 12:3-4

**What would you say to someone who is trying to understand why God created Satan and his demons?**

_____

_____

_____

_____

_____

_____

_____

_____

**Does divisiveness exist in your marriage, in your church, in your relation-ships? How does such an atmosphere cooperate with a demonic agenda?**

_____

_____

_____

_____

_____

_____

_____

## 2. THE NATURE OF DEMONS

We have already seen that God's holy angels are personal beings, and this is true of the fallen angels as well. Luke gives us some insight into the nature of demons:

> "And when He [Jesus] had come out into the land, He was met by a certain man from the city who was possessed with demons; and who had not put on any clothing for a long time, and was not living in a house, but in the tombs. And seeing Jesus, he cried out and fell before Him, and said in a loud voice, "What business do we have with each other, Jesus, Son of the Most High God? I beg You, do not torment me."
>
> Luke 8:27-28

Demons have intellect (they recognized Jesus as the Son of the Most High God), emotions (they said, "Do not torment me"), and will (in verse 32, they requested permission to enter the swine). Intellect, emotions, and will are what make up a person, so demons are not just an ambiguous force blowing in the wind. They are persons, so they understand, talk, communicate and feel.

Not only are demons personal beings, but they are also spiritual beings. Ephesians 6:12 calls them "spiritual forces of wickedness." Because they are spiritual beings, demons cannot be effective unless they are in something else. They cannot achieve their agenda by just flying around. They need a vehicle through which to work, so they use men as their vehicle.

> *"When the unclean spirit goes out of a man, it passes through waterless places seeking rest, and not finding any, it says, 'I will return to my house from which I came.' And when it comes, it finds it swept and put in order. Then it goes and takes along seven other spirits more evil than itself, and they go in and live there; and the last state of that man becomes worse than the first."*
>
> *Luke 11:24-26*

This passage from Luke refers to a man who was possessed by an evil spirit. The spirit left his body, but then became frustrated because there was no place to express itself. So it returned to the man, but not alone; it brought along seven other spirits (worse than the first one).

Because they are spirit beings, demons cannot be effective unless they are in something else.

## Demons are perverted beings. They twist the truth through their own false doctrines.

Demons are also very powerful beings. Luke 8:29 mentions a demon-possessed man who could break free from his own shackles. Perhaps you have heard of this strength when people are on drugs. That's because they're not just on drugs; they're on a demonic vehicle. The Bible describes drugs, sorcery, wizardry, and witchcraft as vehicles that transport demonic activity.

Demons are perverted beings. They twist the truth through their own false doctrines (1 Timothy 4:1). They are also deceitful beings. That's why 1 John 4:1 tells us to "test the spirits" to see if they are from God. The problem is, these perverted demons don't always look perverted. Instead, they disguise themselves as apostles of Christ (2 Corinthians 11:13).

Don't look for two horns, a pitchfork, and a red jumpsuit. Satan and his friends don't want you to know who they are, so they'll come to you disguised as God's servants. That's why you must always measure what you hear by the Word of God.

**Why are demons ineffective unless they are working through a human being?**

_____

_____

_____

_____

_____

_____

**Have you heard any teaching that does not line up with the Bible?**

_____

_____

_____

_____

_____

_____

_____

**How have such "doctrines of demons" perverted the Word of God?**

_____

_____

_____

_____

_____

_____

_____

# 3. THE CATEGORIES OF DEMONS

Satan's demons fall into three specific categories. The first is the most obvious: those who are free to move about at Satan's bidding, to carry out his purposes. The devil cannot be everywhere at one time. He's not omnipresent. He's not omniscient. He's very powerful, but he's not God. So, because he's not God, he needs all these agents to carry out his will. God uses the angels by choice, but Satan has to have them to function.

The second group of demons is permanently imprisoned.

> God uses the angels by choice, but Satan has to have them to function.

*"And angels who did not keep their own domain, but abandoned their proper abode, He has kept in eternal bonds under darkness for the judgment of the great day. Just as Sodom and Gomorrah and the cities around them, since they in the same way as these indulged in gross immorality and went after strange flesh, are exhibited as an example, in undergoing the punishment of eternal fire."*

*Jude 1: 6-7*

The devil cannot be everywhere at one time. He's not omnipresent. He's not omniscient. He's very powerful, but he's not God.

These fallen angels are in permanent bondage because they left their proper abode, which would be the spiritual realm. Because they left their abode, God cast them into eternal fire and eternal judgment. They are locked up with no possibility of release or parole, unlike the first group that is free to do Satan's bidding.

In 2 Peter 2, Peter shows us that God did not spare angels who sinned but cast them into a place where judgment is reserved for them. In Jude, we see that they left their proper abode.

In both places, we see that they committed immorality compared with Sodom and Gomorrah. Second Peter also tells us that this came about in the time of Noah. Back up now to this account in Genesis 6:

*"Now it came about, when men began to multiply on the face of the land, and daughters were born to them, that the sons of God saw that the daughters of men were beautiful; and they took wives for themselves, whomever they chose. Then the Lord said,*

> 'My Spirit shall not strive with man forever, because he also is flesh; nevertheless his days shall be one hundred and twenty years.' The Nephilim were on the earth in those days, and also afterward, when the sons of God came into the daughters of men, and they bore children to them. Those were the mighty men who were of old, men of renown."
>
> *Genesis 6:1-4*

To understand this passage, we have to compare it with what we have already seen in the New Testament. Angels, Jude says, left their first abode to come down to earth and commit immorality. Peter says this produced the judgment by flood in the time of Noah. Genesis fills in the rest of the puzzle.

The sons of God, another term for angels, took up residence within wicked men. Because they were demons, they were able to enter the men's bodies and have sexual relationships with the daughters of men. Why would they do that? It all goes back to the angelic conflict. Satan was told that he would be defeated by the seed of a woman (Genesis 3:15).

The devil cannot be everywhere at one time. He's not omnipresent. He's not omniscient. He's very powerful, but he's not God.

Satan did not want this Baby to be born, so he came up with a plan to control all the births; the satanically inspired relationships between the sons of God. Satan thought he had scored a technical victory. There was only one problem: "Noah found favor in the eyes of the Lord" (Genesis 6:8). God can always find one, and He found Noah. So God took one family and one seed and started all over again.

The first group of demonic angels is free to move about at Satan's command. The second group was risked and lost, because God has reserved for those demons a permanent place of incarceration until Judgment Day.

There is one more group, and in this group the demons are temporarily incarcerated. "And they were entreating Him not to command them to depart into the abyss" (Luke 8:31). They were afraid that Jesus would exile them to the abyss, therefore putting them out of commission.

Angels left their first abode to come down to earth and commit immorality. This produced the judgment by flood in the time of Noah.

**How did God respond when the angels left their abode and crossed the line? Why do you think the demons stayed away from Noah? Read Genesis 6:8 9 before you answer.**

_____

_____

_____

_____

_____

_____

_____

## 4. THE SPHERES OF DEMONS

Demons want to destroy four things. First of all, they want to destroy you. First Peter 5:8 says Satan is like a "roaring lion, seeking someone to devour." Satan wants you, and he will try to get you any way he can. The will of Satan is to keep the unsaved blind and the saved ineffective.

Second, he wants your family. That's what he went after in Genesis 6. The sons of God came down and destroyed the family. There was only one family left. Satan and his army want access to your family so that they can destroy the communication in your home.

Third, Satan wants to destroy the church. He was able to find a way into the lives of Ananias and Sapphira, convincing them to lie and steal from God (Acts 5).

And finally, He wants to destroy society. Daniel 10:13 says nations are controlled by demons, so the political realm can be demonized. That's why the impact of God's people is so important in society.

If we're going to keep Satan out of our lives, then we have to remember the words of Matthew 12:29: "Or how can anyone enter the strong man's house and carry off his property, unless he first binds the strong man? And then he will plunder his house." If you're a believer in Jesus Christ, the Holy Spirit lives within you.

> Satan wants you, and he will try to get you any way he can. The will of Satan is to keep the unsaved blind and the saved ineffective.

There's no binding that strong man, because he's too strong. As the Scripture says, "Greater is He who is in you than he who is in the world" (I John 4:4). If you belong to Jesus, you're on the winning side—because you're now seated in heavenly places too (Ephesians 2:6).

**What are three specific ways you can fight to keep Satan's influence out of your home? What are three specific ways you can fight to keep Satan's influence out of your church?**

_____

_____

_____

_____

_____

_____

_____

_____

_____

If you're a believer in Jesus Christ, the Holy Spirit liv within you. There's no binding Him, because He's too strong.

# NOTES

# LESSON 6

## THE PROGRAM OF DEMONS

*Satan...* is like a Mafia godfather who oversees a vast number of demonic beings that influence men in order to carry out their master's agenda. This spiritual Mafia is very important to him because, unlike God, the devil is not omnipresent, omnipotent, or omniscient. Therefore these special agents are not a choice but a necessity.

> Demons want to remove purity of life because God's central characteristic is His holiness.

Understanding how demons work will help to equip us for spiritual warfare against the enemy. The program of demons is like a two-sided-coin in one hand, the goal is to promote Satan; in the other hand, the goal is to oppose God.

## 1. DEMONS PROMOTE FALSE DOCTRINE

Satan's demons want to teach their master's lies disseminating their information into the minds of men so that men might live according to Satan's theology rather than God's.

*"But the Spirit explicitly says that in later times some will fall away from the faith, paying attention to deceitful spirits and doctrines of demons."*

1 Timothy 4:1

False doctrines are always designed to undermine truth. The first doctrine that the demons propagate is that God is not good. The first words of the serpent are recorded in Genesis 3:1, where he questions the word of God:

*"And he said to the woman, indeed, has God said, 'you shall not eat from any tree of the garden?'"*

There are certain things we cannot do as Christians, but the "I cant's" are not the essence of Christianity.

Teachers can undermine the goodness of God by focusing on the "I cant's" of Christianity. According to 1 Timothy 4:3, false teachers were forbidding marriage and encouraging people to abstain from certain foods. Anyone who focuses on the "I cant's" is promoting a doctrine from hell.

There are certain things we cannot do as Christians, but the "I cant's" are not the essence of Christianity. The essence of Christianity is all that God has freely given us to enjoy. Satan wants to point out the one tree we can't have instead of the thousands we can have. He wants to explain God as one who does not want us to enjoy life, and that's just not true.

Not only does demonic doctrine attempt to undermine the goodness of God, but it also wants to undermine the Son of God. Paul warned the Corinthians in 2 Corinthians 11:3 that there are people who are willing to lead us astray from the simplicity and purity of devotion to Christ. The reason we must be careful here is that false teachers don't advertise the fact that they're promoting lies (2 Corinthians 11:13-15). The demons know that as long as Christ is in the center of our lives, they cannot dominate and control us.

The third way demonic doctrine attempts to pervert the truth is by undermining the gospel. Satan wants to put blinders on the unrighteous so that they will remain in their sins (2 Corinthians 4:3-4).

**Read Genesis 3:1 again. Note the serpent's first four words. What was he saying to Eve?**

_____

_____

_____

_____

_____

_____

_____

_____

_____

**Read Ephesians 2:8-10. According to this passage, how are we saved?**

_____

_____

_____

_____

_____

_____

_____

_____

_____

**How would a "salvation by works" doctrine blind a person to truth?**

_____

_____

_____

_____

_____

_____

_____

_____

_____

## 2. DEMONS PROMOTE DESTRUCTION

The demonic angels also promote their leader by pushing his formula for destruction. Satan is about destroying, killing, and bringing great harm to men and women. The New Testament is full of examples of how demonic forces have succeeded in greatly debilitating people.

Satan is not responsible for every single illness or sickness. However, there are many more physical and emotional illnesses that are demonically orchestrated than we usually give the demons credit for. Why? Because demons disguise themselves as angels of light. They don't want us to see that they're behind our problems.

Satan is about destroying, killing, and bringing great harm to men and women. When something goes wrong in our lives, Jesus Christ is the first place, not the last place, we should turn.

THE PROGRAM OF DEMONS

In Matthew 12:22, Jesus met a man whose blindness was caused by demons:

*"Then a demon-possessed man who was blind and mute was brought to Jesus, and He healed him, so that the mute man spoke and saw."*

Verse 24 reveals that Jesus healed him by getting rid of his spiritual problem. Also in Matthew, Jesus cast out a demon from a mute man so that the man could speak again (Matthew 9:32-33).

Demons are also sometimes responsible for physical deformity. Jesus healed a woman who had been bent over for 18 years because of a spirit (Luke 13:11-13). Demons can also create emotional instability and insanity. One example is found in Matthew 17. A man begged the Lord to heal his lunatic son who was very ill. The boy would often fall into the fire or fall into the water, threatening his very life (vs. 14-18).

We have already studied the account of the demon-possessed man who lived in the tombs. A naked man living among the dead does not have all of his mental faculties (Luke 8:26-33). When something goes wrong in our lives, Jesus Christ is the first place—not the last place—we should turn.

**Why is it significant to know if an ailment has a physical or spiritual cause?**

_____

_____

_____

_____

_____

_____

**Have you or someone you know experienced an illness the doctors can't detect? Could the cause be spiritual?**

_____

_____

_____

_____

_____

_____

_____

## 3. DEMONS PROMOTE DOMINATION

Another goal of the devil is the domination of the whole world. He wants to bring down nations by influencing political leaders. God's angel was trying to reach Daniel in Daniel 10:13-20, but was blocked by demonic forces wanting to control the political realm of Persia.

The degree to which demonic influences control a society, an environment, or a family is the degree to which we will not be able to enjoy and see the blessings of God. This is evident all around the world, especially in countries that are mired in witchcraft and sorcery. Once the devil dominates, there can be no progress.

**In what ways can you see demonic forces influencing your country? Think of at least two examples of how your government or its leaders are opposing the Word of God?**

_____

_____

_____

_____

_____

_____

_____

_____

**Based on what you have studied, what are some doctrines you would expect to hear in a church that is influenced by Satan's demons?**

_____

_____

_____

_____

_____

_____

_____

_____

# 4. DEMONS PROMOTE DISTRACTION

Far too many Christians are unclear on the distractions that demons bring about when they lure us away from a centralized focus on God.

Leviticus 19:31 says,

> *"Do not turn to mediums or spirits; do not seek them out to be defiled by them. I am the Lord your God."*

The degree to which demonic influences control a society, an environment, or a family is the degree to which we will not be able to enjoy and see the blessings of God.

Whenever you appeal to the created world to do what is the prerogative of the Creator, you have changed gods. You have allowed yourself to become distracted from the one true God. "As for the person who turns to mediums and to spirits, to play the harlot after them, I will set my face against that person and will cut him off from among his people" (Leviticus 20:6).

When you dabble in the occult, you are dabbling in that which compromises, distracts you from, and plays games with the centrality of God. Those who belong to Him are not to do it.

> When you enter the land which the Lord your God gives you, you shall not learn to imitate the detestable things of those nations. There shall not be found among you anyone who makes his son or his daughter pass through the fire, one who uses divination, one who practices witch-craft, or one who interprets omens, or a sorcerer, or one who casts a spell, or a medium, or spirits, or one who calls up the dead. For whoever does these things is detestable to the Lord; and because of these detestable things the Lord your God will drive them out before you. You shall be blameless before the Lord your God.
>
> Deuteronomy 18:9-13

If you have dabbled in any of these areas that the Bible forbids, if you have called a psychic hot-line, or if you have read your horoscope in the newspaper, then you have opened the door to the possibility of demonic influence in your life. Go to God in prayer, asking Him to forgive you and to deliver you from any satanic influence in your life.

**If we are believers, then we are complete in Christ (Colossians 2:10). We don't need an intermediary to look into our future. What is distracting you from your focus on Him?**

_____

_____

_____

_____

_____

_____

_____

**Read Acts 19:17-20. What did the people do when they realized the error of their ways?**

_____

_____

_____

_____

_____

_____

_____

## 5. DEMONS OPPOSE GOD'S POSITION

Satan's regime is hard at work to promote evil and wickedness in the physical and visible world, but promoting evil is not the only task at hand. Demons also stay busy opposing God. One of the primary ways they oppose God's agenda is through encouraging idolatry among men and women.

> They made Him jealous with strange gods; with abominations they provoked Him to anger. They sacrificed to demons who were not God, to gods whom they have not known, new gods who came lately, whom your fathers did not dread.
>
> *Deuteronomy 32:16-17*

Watch out for "new gods." Though they thought they were sacrificing to idols, they were actually sacrificing to demons. Behind every idol is a demon. And this is not just in the Old Testament. Read what the New Testament says about sacrificing to idols:

> *No, but I say that the things which the Gentiles sacrifice, they sacrifice to demons, and not to God; and I do not want you to become sharers in demons. You cannot drink the cup of the Lord and the cup of demons; you cannot partake of the table of the Lord and the table of demons. Or do we provoke the Lord to jealousy? We are not stronger than He, are we?*
>
> *1 Corinthians 10:20-22*

Watch out for
"new gods."
Behind every
idol is a demon.

Paul is writing to a New Testament church that is taking communion. And he explains that there are two tables: the Lord's table and the demons' table. Whenever you partake of an idol that belongs to the unsaved, unbelieving, godless world and when you let their idol become your idol, you share in their fellowship. If you are partaking of idols, then you are losing out on fellowship with God. By adopting fellowship with them, you are adopting fellowship with their gods or demons.

**What, if anything, is distracting you from making God the center of your life?**

_____

_____

_____

_____

_____

_____

# 6. DEMONS OPPOSE GOD'S PURITY

Jude gives us some insight into the angels that stepped over the line in Genesis. God has permanently incarcerated these angels because of the gross immorality. Demons had been behind ungodly relationships that produced the Nephilim.

> Demons want to remove purity of life because God's central characteristic is His holiness.

Demons want to remove purity of life because God's central characteristic is His holiness. And without purity, there is no fellowship with God; you must get rid of the impurity. The only thing that can get rid of the impurity is the blood of Jesus Christ.

**Are you maintaining moral purity in your walk with the Lord?**

_____

_____

_____

_____

_____

_____

_____

**Read Hebrews 13:4. Why do Satan's demons so strongly oppose God's purity?**

_____

_____

_____

_____

_____

_____

_____

## 7. DEMONS OPPOSE GOD'S PEOPLE

Finally, hell's demons oppose the people of God. Satan opposes us by slandering us to God. In Revelation 12:10, he is called the accuser of the brethren. He delights in exposing all of our sins because he knows God must judge sin.

> Demons know what they're doing. They are not a house divided. Their strength is in their unity. They operate as one.

They operate as one. If we would operate as one in our relationship with God, our families, and our churches, there would be no room for demons in our lives. Demons have to be able to divide us before they can be successful.

Remember, we are not alone. In that same courtroom where Satan accuses us day and night, we also have an Advocate with the Father—Jesus Christ. He is on our side, and is a constant reminder that He has paid our debt and secured for us a full pardon.

**Read Romans 8:31-39. How do you intend to stand against Satanic opposition?**

_____

_____

_____

_____

_____

# NOTES

# LESSON 7

## THE DOMINATION OF DEMONS

*Satan's goal...* is to dominate people's lives, and he accomplishes this domination through the assistance of his demons. They work in one of two ways: oppression or possession.

> The devil's ultimate objective is demon possession. But if he cannot get that far, then he will seek to dominate by oppression.

The devil's ultimate objective is demon possession. But if he cannot get that far, then he will seek to dominate by oppression. In this way, he will make life so miserable, so uncomfortable, and so destructive that, even though he doesn't live inside of you, he orchestrates your circumstances so that life becomes overwhelmingly problematic.

In order to understand the schemes of the devil, four aspects of demonic domination should be studied, including a definition of domination, its distinctive characteristics, its devices, and deliverance from it.

# 1. DEMONIC DOMINATION: A DEFINITION

Demonic domination, or demonization, is the occupation of a human being by one or more evil spirits. These spirits occupy a human in order to exercise various levels of control over that person. They want to control physically, psychologically, and spiritually.

> *And when He had come out of the boat, immediately a man from the tombs with an unclean spirit met Him.*
>
> Mark 5:2

In fact, many demons had entered him (Luke 8:30). This man was totally controlled by demons, for their ultimate goal is to move from mere oppression to possession. They want to make life so miserable that they can completely conquer someone's personality, bringing it into subjection to their goals and agendas.

Demons want to occupy a body. They want to overrun the person and the personality. They can bring all kinds of misery to a body without causing suspicion. Satan is a great counterfeiter, and he wants others to think that the problem is either purely physical or purely psychological.

**What would be the difference between someone who is oppressed by a demon and someone who is possessed by a demon?**

_____

_____

_____

_____

_____

_____

_____

_____

## 2. DEMONIC DOMINATION: DISTINCTIVE CHARACTERISTICS

Oppression and possession do offer distinctive characteristics that might alert someone who is sensitive to the invisible spiritual realm.

One of the characteristics of people who are demon-possessed is an increase in physical strength. The demon-possessed man in Mark 5:3-4 was able to rip apart his own chains. People who are demon-possessed have unusual strength because they are borrowing that strength from the fallen angelic being operating inside of them.

> Oppression and possession do offer distinctive characteristics that might alert someone who is sensitive to the invisible, spiritual realm.

When people are high on drugs, they sometimes display unusual strength, and it's because demons ride the backs of drugs. Drug addiction is one of the mechanisms Satan's forces use to infiltrate and possess people.

Demon possession can also manifest itself in fits of rage. The demoniac in Mark 5:4 must have been docile enough at one point to allow the others to shackle him, but he then broke the shackles and chains in a fit of rage.

A split personality can be another sign of demon possession. Again, this passage in Mark is our model because it makes such a comprehensive statement on demonology. In verses 6 and 7, the man sees Jesus from a distance, runs up and bows down before Him, then cries out, "Do not torment me!" Recognizing Jesus, bowing down before Him, and then begging Him not to torment you is contradictory behavior. Demonic possession can cause schizophrenia in a person when another being has made itself at home and is influencing that person.

Those who have been possessed by demons will resist spiritual things. Notice in verse 7 that, though the man acknowledges Jesus as the Son of the Most High God, he wants to be left alone. The demons know who Jesus is, and He makes them very uncomfortable.

Then there's a different voice that can come out of one who is possessed by a demon.

> *"And He was asking him, 'What is your name?' And he said to Him, 'My name is Legion; for we are many'" (v. 9).*

Legion was the name for a Roman army with 6,000 to 12,000 soldiers. In essence, this demon was saying, "There are more than 6,000 of us inside of this guy." How could that many get inside one being? They're spiritual beings, and they don't have the same space limitations as we do. So demons were speaking through this man.

> When people are high on drugs they sometimes display unusual strength, and its' because demons ride the backs of drugs.

Another distinctive characteristic of demon possession is transference. The demons in Mark 5 were begging Jesus not to send them out of the country because they had assigned responsibilities in this place, and He allowed them to go from the man's body into the swine.

A herd of 2,000 pigs was grazing nearby. When the demons entered the pigs, they went berserk and plunged off the bank into the sea. So the ability to transfer from one place to another is possible. However, note that they could only leave in this case with Jesus' permission. Jesus Christ has authority.

> God responded to belief and overran the un-belief, because this man had enough belief to come to the right Person.

Demons can also manifest themselves in ways that are normally viewed as physical, psychological, or spiritual. Mark tells the story of a boy who was mute and would try to kill himself (9:17-18). The boy would fall to the ground, foam at the mouth, grind his teeth, and then stiffen out. The father said to Jesus,

*"If You can do anything, take pity on us and help us!" And Jesus said to him, "If You can! All things are possible to him who believes." Immediately the boy's father cried out and began saying, "I do believe; help my unbelief."*
*Mark 9:22-24*

That's good news. Jesus said, "If you believe, all things are possible. Do you believe?" The man basically answered, "Kinda." He said, "I do believe; help my unbelief." God responded to the belief and overran the unbelief, because this man had enough belief to come to the right Person.

**What makes the characteristics of the demon-possessed person so distinctive?**

_____

_____

_____

_____

_____

_____

_____

_____

**Do you think there is hope for someone who is oppressed or possessed by demons? Thinking back to Jesus' earthly ministry, how would you answer?**

_____

_____

_____

_____

_____

_____

_____

_____

## 3. DEMONIC DOMINATION DEVICES USED

Satan's angels want to take possession of human beings, and there are several devices that allow possession or oppression to take place. However, we can control many of those devices.

One of the main ways demons gain entry into a person's life is through idolatry. Behind every idol is a demon. This is critical.

> _"Therefore, my beloved, flee from idolatry… Is not the cup of blessing which we bless a sharing in the blood of Christ? Is not the bread which we break a sharing in the body of Christ?"_
>
> _1 Corinthians 10:14, 16_

One of the main ways demons gain entry into a person's life is through idolatry.

Communion is not a time where we just remember the past. When we partake of communion, we are participating in the life of Jesus Christ. Now read verses 19 and 20:

*"What do I mean then? That a thing sacrificed to idols is anything, or that an idol is anything? No, but I say that the things which the Gentiles sacrifice, they sacrifice to demons, and not to God; and I do not want you to become sharers in demons."*

Communion is not a time where we just remember the past. When we partake of communion, we are participating in the life of Jesus Christ.

Paul is writing to Christians, telling us that when we participate with non-Christians in their idolatry, it's like taking the bread and the cup of communion and, instead of participating in the life of Christ, participating in the life of demons.

When we worship idols, we become tools in the hands of the devil and open ourselves up for either oppression or possession. There is a debate among Christians on the question of whether a believer can be possessed, but the answer to that question is irrelevant to this study. Possession is bad, and oppression is bad enough. So, whether oppressed or possessed, the point is that we must get Satan and his demons out of our neighborhoods.

Another way demons gain access is through a person's participation in the occult. This involves astrology, horoscopes, palm reading, psychic predictions, and a whole lot more. You may think these things are harmless, but they are a vehicle by which Satan can drive right into your life.

Spiritual immaturity can also open you up to demonic influence. As Satanic doctrines creep into the church, those who have not developed spiritual discernment are easy prey for false teaching.

Because these people do not know the way of God, they can easily be duped by the lies of the devil.

Drug use is another vehicle Satan uses to infiltrate lives. In Galatians 5:20, the word sorcery is the Greek word pharmakeict, which refers to drug use. Satan uses this to his advantage because drug use dulls the personality. Anytime the personality and the mind are dulled, demonic influences can walk right in.

> Anytime the personality and the mind are dulled, demonic influences can walk right in.

We have also seen how sexual immorality can give the devil some headway into the lives of human beings. In Genesis 6, the merger between the sons of God and the daughters of men was a promotion of sexual immorality so that Satan and his angels could control and dominate.

**Have you in any way allowed Satan access to your life? Have you allowed any idol to take God's place in your life?**

_____

_____

_____

_____

_____

_____

_____

**Are you a Christian who has not been maturing spiritually? Do you want the perks of salvation without getting to know your God?**

_____

_____

_____

_____

_____

_____

# 4. DEMONIC DOMINATION: DELIVERANCE

Before we can overcome demonism in our lives or help somebody we know overcome demonism in theirs, we must first understand three things.

First, we must understand the authority of Christ. Do you remember the controversy that erupted when Jesus cast out a demon in Matthew 12? Some people accused him of casting out the demon through Satan's power. Jesus then pointed out the absurdity of their statement, because His power was revealing His authority as the Christ, the Son of God.

Jesus Christ has defeated Satan and his demons by means of the cross.

> Only in the authority of Christ can we find the authority to deal with our demons and help others deal with theirs. We must view ourselves through our new position in Christ, not our old position in Adam.

Satan was about to be cast out when Jesus was about to be lifted up. When He was lifted up on the cross, Satan got booted out.

Only in the authority of Christ can we find the authority to deal with our demons and help others deal with theirs. We must view ourselves through our new position in Christ, not our old position in Adam.

The second thing we have to understand is the authority of the believer. As Christians, we have authority granted by Jesus Himself.

> *"And having summoned His twelve disciples, He gave them authority over unclean spirits, to cast them out, and to heal every kind of disease and every kind of sickness."*
>
> Matthew 10:1

Jesus' authority was not only given to the 12 disciples, but to the whole church.

*And I also say to you that you are Peter, and upon this rock I will build My church; and the gates of Hades shall not overpower it. I will give you the keys of the kingdom of heaven; and whatever you shall bind on earth shall be bound in heaven, and whatever you shall loose on earth shall be loosed in heaven.*

Matthew 16:18-19

> If you are a fence-walking, tightrope-walking Christian, then you are in great danger of becoming a candidate for the demonic realm. The holiness of God demands that you get off the fence.

The last thing we must understand in avoiding the enemy's domination is our personal responsibility. We are responsible for deciding right now that we will not compromise our faith, that we will commit ourselves to prayer, and that we will remove from our lives any remnant of the occult.

There is absolutely no room in the believer's life for spiritual compromise. If you are a fence-walking, tightrope-walking Christian, then you are in great danger of becoming a candidate for the demonic realm. The holiness of God demands that you get off the fence.

Remember the book-burning in Acts 19? Maybe it's time you went home and burned up every little trinket, every little horoscope, every little demonic card you have. You may have a whole host of demons circling your home because they feel comfortable there. You need to take everything that is connected to Satan and get it out of your house—immediately.

In Matthew 12:43-45, an evil spirit left a man, then changed his mind. When he got back, the man had wept and cleaned up. Somehow, the guy had bettered his situation.

There's only one problem—the house was still unoccupied. If you leave your house unoccupied, no matter how much you sweep it and clean it up, if you let that thing just sit there unoccupied, somebody is going to lay claim to it. And if somebody doesn't lay claim to it, it's still going to deteriorate. It must be occupied to be kept up. If Jesus Christ does not occupy you, you're in trouble.

He wants to take up residence inside of you, but He won't come without an invitation. If you really want Him, and if you ask Him, He'll come in right now and never, never leave.

**Does demonic domination scare you? In this study, you must not forget that Jesus has already won this war. Read Hebrews 2:14–15 and 1 Peter 3:22.**

_____

_____

_____

_____

_____

_____

_____

_____

Is there anything at all in your home that does not honor God? Today is the day for you to get rid of it. Read Acts 19 and pray that God would show you if you have any "magic books" that need to be burned.

If Jesus Christ does not occupy you, you're in trouble. He wants to take up residence inside of you, but He won't come without an invitation.

# NOTES

# LESSON 8

## THE DOCTRINE OF DEMONS

*In his first letter...* to Timothy, Paul makes a
*direct correlation between an attitude of thanksgiving and demonic activity.*

> For everything created by God is good...
> 1 Timothy 4:4

*"But the Spirit explicitly says that in later times some will fall away from the faith, paying attention to deceitful spirits and doctrines of demons, by means of the hypocrisy of liars seared in their own conscience as with a branding iron, men who forbid marriage and advocate abstaining from foods, which God has created to be gratefully shared in by those who believe and know the truth. For everything created by God is good, and nothing is to be rejected, if it is received with gratitude; for it is sanctified by means of the word of God and prayer."*

*1 Timothy 4:1-5*

In making this correlation between ingratitude and demonic activity, what he is saying is that if you are an ungrateful person and especially an ungrateful Christian, then you are living under demonic influence.

# 1. THE PROBLEM OF THANKSGIVING

Satan designed his doctrine of demons in order to cause us to lose sight of the goodness of God. When we fail to see the goodness of God in every circumstance of life, then we become ungrateful and thus open ourselves up to demonic influence in our lives.

In the passage from 1 Timothy, the false teachers (themselves under the influence of demons) were keeping Christians from fully enjoying what God had provided. A lot of Christians don't get a chance to give thanks because they're not enjoying everything God has given them. If your Christian life is negative, and if your Christian life is measured only by what you can't do now that you're a Christian, then you have been duped by demons.

The Christian life should be made up more of what you do enjoy under God, rather than what you can't enjoy under God. Losing sight of His goodness is a problem, because we're not inclined to give thanks to a God who does not appear to be good. In fact, if we believe God is not a good God, we're inclined to go to the other extreme, as in Romans 1:18-23:

For everything created by God is good, and nothing is to be rejected, if it is received with gratitude, for it is sanctified by means of the word of God and prayer.
1 Timothy 4:4-5

"For the wrath of God is revealed from heaven against all ungodliness and unrighteousness of men, who suppress the truth in unrighteousness, because that which is known about God is evident within them; for God made it evident to them. For since the creation of the world His invisible attributes, His eternal power and divine nature, have been clear-

*ly seen, being understood through what has been made, so that they are without excuse. For even though they knew God, they did not honor him as God, or give thanks; but they became futile in their speculations, and their foolish heart was darkened. Professing to be wise, they became fools, and exchanged the glory of the incorruptible God for an image in the form of corruptible man and of birds and four-footed animals and crawling creatures."*

That passage goes on to say that they worshiped and served the creature instead of worshiping and serving the Creator who created the creature. That's idolatry. And remember, behind every idol is a demon.

The absence of gratitude is dangerous because of its link to idolatry. Our God is a jealous God, and He will not tolerate idols in our lives (see Deuteronomy 6:10-15).

God wants us to be grateful for all that He has given us. But He doesn't just want to hear 'thank You, thank You, thank You, thank You." He wants you to have a grateful heart that will allow you to see past the doctrine of the demons.

**Does your religion so burden you with what you can't do that you are unable to enjoy all that God has given you? Ask God to show you, through His Spirit, if those "you can'ts" are from His Word or from a demonically influenced legalism.**

**Do you sometimes struggle with the goodness of God? In a world that is full of violence, suffering, and unimaginable horror, how do you know you can trust His goodness? Read Exodus 34:6; Psalm 31:19; 52:1; 65:4; 145:9. Record your response here.**

_____

_____

_____

_____

_____

_____

_____

_____

_____

_____

**List below what you learned from them, then keep these truths close to your heart.**

_____

_____

_____

_____

_____

_____

_____

_____

The Christian life should be made up more of what you do enjoy under God rather than what you can't enjoy under God. Losing sight of His goodness is a problem, because we're not inclined to give thanks to a God who does not appear to be good.

## 2. THE PRIORITY OF THANKSGIVING

Paul says in the second half of 1 Timothy 4:3, "which God has created to be gratefully shared in by those who believe and know the truth." That's a powerful verse.

The most grateful people in the whole world, according to verse 3, should be those who believe and know the truth. Paul says those Christians who really know who God is and what God does and has done, ought to be the most grateful people around.

> The most grateful people in the whole world should be those who believe and know the truth.

What most people want today is the goodies of God without being grateful to the God from whom the goodies come. But there is nothing that we enjoy that cannot be traced back to God. If you are enjoying the home you're living in, then think about where that wood came from. If you're enjoying the money in your wallet or purse, then think about where the paper for that money came from.

Everything can be traced back to the provision of God. As believers, showing our gratitude to God should be the highest priority of our lives.

A classic example of gratitude is seen in Luke 17:11-19. Ten men were miserable because they had the debilitating, ultimately fatal disease of leprosy, which is a sort of cancer that causes a person to lose feeling in the limbs. Eventually, the fingers and hands waste away. It is a terrible disease. But then Jesus came along.

> Whenever we love the blessing more than the God who blesses, we're committing idolatry.

The men cried out to Him to have mercy on them. He responded by healing all 10 men. Excited and anxious to tell everyone the good news, they forgot all about the One who had healed them. Then one man stopped in his tracks. He ran back to Jesus, fell on his face before Him, and thanked Him. Jesus asked him, "Were there not ten cleansed? But the nine—where are they?" (v. 17).

Where were they? Where did they go? They were so busy enjoying the blessing of God that they forgot the God who blessed. They were so busy enjoying the goodness of God that they forgot the God who had been good.

Whenever we love the blessing more than the God who blesses, we're committing idolatry. We are then worshiping the gift instead of the Giver. Many of us are not getting more from God because He's not about to give us more for which we will forget to say thanks.

**Read Ephesians 5:20 and 1 Thessalonians 5:18. According to these passages, when should we be prepared to give thanks?**

_____

_____

_____

_____

_____

_____

_____

_____

**Do you say thanks as a way of life? Or are you becoming an idolater and allowing yourself to be influenced by Satan's demons?**

_____

_____

_____

_____

_____

_____

_____

_____

# 3. THE PROVISION OF THANKSGIVING

God has provided countless reasons for us to give thanks to Him. He has made it easy for us to receive with gratitude all of His many blessings. God doesn't make junk, so everything that comes from Him is good.

> It's important to realize that goodness has to do with intrinsic quality, not external enjoyment.

Now, it's important to realize that goodness has to do with intrinsic quality, not external enjoyment. That's a fundamental distinction. When the Bible talks about good, it talks about what is beneficial, not simply that which is enjoyable. Unrighteous man measures good by "Do I like it?" "Did I enjoy it?" "Was it fun?" "If it was, it must be good." No. In the Bible, good has to do with intrinsic benefit, not merely external enjoyment.

Romans 8:28 says,

> _"And we know that God causes all things to work together for good to those who love God, to those who are called according to His purpose."_

It's not that everything that happens is fun, but it's that anything God does in our lives has benefit to it. Therefore, it is intrinsically good.

There are some valuable insights into the provision of God in James 1:17:

> *"Every good thing bestowed and every perfect gift is from above, coming down from the Father of lights, with whom there is no variation, or shifting shadow."*

He says a number of things in this verse. First of all, what comes from God to you is like what comes from a father to a son or daughter. So He's talking about relational gifts. And we know that parents who love their children give them things that are beneficial to them even though sometimes those things are painful. When you take your child to the doctor for a shot, the needle is painful but good and necessary for the child. It didn't feel good, but it was beneficial. Now, He's the Father of lights, and with Him there is no variation or shifting shadow.

Because we are expected to give thanks, God has made provision for our thanksgiving. In light of that, it's so important that we honor Him for the things that come into our lives.

What does that mean? Think about how the earth rotates around the sun. As it rotates, part of its surface is facing the sun and part of its surface is turned away from the sun. The earth changes, and therefore a shadow or darkness comes across the earth. The sun does not change; it's still full of light. James is saying that God is immutable—He does not change.

Giving thanks always points us back to God, regardless of our circumstances. When Jerusalem was falling apart in the book of Lamentations, Jeremiah said, "Great is Thy faithfulness" (Lamentations 3:23). And remember Matthew Henry's story? After being robbed, he said to God, "I want to thank you that even though he took all I had, I didn't have much." Can you see how "in everything giving thanks" changes one's perspective? Because we are expected to give thanks, God has made provision for our thanksgiving.

In light of that, it's so important that we honor Him for the things that come into our lives. "Instruct those who are rich in this present world not to be conceited or to fix their hope on the uncertainty of riches, but on God, who richly supplies us with all things to enjoy" (1 Timothy 6:17).

> The Father of lights never turns. We are the ones who turn from Him.

We are to fix our hope where? On God. Why? He richly supplies us with all things to enjoy. If your trust is in your bank account, it's in the wrong place. If your trust is in stocks and bonds, it's in the wrong place. If your trust is in your house, it's in the wrong place. Your focus must not be on the gift but on the Giver. The provision of thanksgiving to counteract the doctrine of demons is to say, "God, I give You glory."

# 4. THE POWER OF THANKSGIVING

First Timothy 4:5 says,

*"For it is sanctified by means of the word of God and prayer."*

The Greek word for sanctified means "set apart, consecrated, dedicated." If you sanctify something, you set it apart for God's special use.

You can always test what comes into your life by two things: the Word of God and prayer. Let's start with the Word. If a bank robber says, "Well, this money came from God," he's wrong. How can we be sure? Because the Bible says,

"You shall not steal." The Word of God provides boundaries to let you know whether what you're receiving is authentic or not.

What this verse in 1 Timothy is saying is that when God gives something that's good, substantiated by the Word of God and prayer, ordinary things become extraordinary. When you take the things that God gives you and then give God the glory He deserves, then He touches the ordinary and makes it extraordinary.

If your trust is in your bank account, it's in the wrong place. If your trust is in stocks and bonds, it's in the wrong place. If your trust is in your house, it's in the wrong place.

You know the story, but let's look at it one more time. We need to see why an ordinary lunch is remembered as an extraordinary lunch.

*"Jesus therefore lifting up His eyes, and seeing that a great multitude was coming to Him, said to Philip, 'Where are we to buy bread, that these may eat?' . . . Philip answered Him, 'Two hundred denarii worth of bread is not sufficient for them, for everyone to receive a little.' One of His disciples, Andrew, Simon Peter's brother, said to Him, 'There is a lad here who has five barley loaves and two fish, but what are these for so many people?' . . . Jesus therefore took the loaves; and having given thanks, He distributed to those who were seated; likewise also of the fish as much as they wanted. And when they were filled, He said to His disciples, 'Gather up the leftover fragments that nothing may be lost.' And so they gathered them up, and filled twelve baskets with fragments from the five barley loaves, which were left over by those who had eaten."*

*John 6:5, 7-9, 11-13*

Think about past circumstances in your life. Can you see how God used what was not enjoyable to benefit you in your spiritual growth? Read Romans 8:28-30. What does verse 29 say about the purpose of trials?

_____

_____

_____

_____

_____

_____

_____

The Father of lights never turns. We are the ones who turn from Him. Where are you standing in relation to the Son? Why don't you say a prayer of thanksgiving right now?

_____

_____

_____

_____

_____

_____

Read 1 Chronicles 16:7-36. Make this your prayer to God. Maybe your situation is so terrible that you can't understand why God allows it. Regardless of what your circumstances look like, you must cling to His Word. The Bible says He is good, so thank Him.

_____

_____

_____

_____

_____

_____

_____

Psalm 100 would be a great chapter for you to memorize. It's only five short verses. Read this Psalm and repeat it back to God.

Maybe you're still thinking, "But you don't understand! Everything is wrong in my life!" God knows all about it, and He's in control. You need to praise Him.

If you increase thanksgiving and decrease complaining, your circumstances will begin to change. When you increase complaining and don't enjoy what God has given you, you have adopted the doctrine of demons—idolatry.

# NOTES

# LESSON 9

## THE REBELLION OF SATAN

*We have seen...*that there is an invisible, spiritual realm that influences the visible, physical realm. We have seen that this world is run by angels. We have looked at the origins of angels and demons, we have looked at their activities, and we have looked at their goals.

> The Bible says we are in a conflict with spiritual forces of wickedness.

We have seen that as the holy angels dedicate themselves to carrying out the will of God in our lives, the fallen angels, or demons, dedicate themselves to promoting the agenda of Satan. Now we're going to take a closer look at the leader of this demonic regime, the devil.

The Bible says we are in a conflict with spiritual forces of wickedness. We must engage ourselves in spiritual warfare. As Christians, we already have the necessary weapons for the battle. But it's important to understand who we're up against so that we can fight this war intelligently.

# 1. THE CAUSE OF SATAN'S REBELLION

Before we can understand why Satan would rebel against God, we need to look at where he was and what he was doing in his original capacity.

Ezekiel 28 begins with God telling Ezekiel to speak to the leader of Tyre, a ruler who was seeking to live independently of God. But in verse 12, God told him to take up a lamentation over the king of Tyre. Remember how the spiritual world parallels the physical world? Behind the earthly leader of Tyre was a spiritual king-Satan.

At the beginning of his life, Satan was a flawless being. There was not a scratch to be found on him.

When God created Satan, He created him in perfection. Let's look at those perfections.

*"Son of man, take up a lamentation over the king of Tyre, and say to him, Thus says the Lord God, 'You had the seal of perfection, full of wisdom and perfect in beauty. You were in Eden, the garden of God; every precious stone was your covering; the ruby, the topaz, and the diamond; the beryl, the onyx and the jasper; the lapis lazuli, the turquoise, and the emerald; and the gold, the workmanship of your settings and sockets, was in you. On the day that you were created they were prepared.'"*

*Ezekiel 28:12-13*

At the beginning of his life, Satan was a flawless being. There was not a scratch to be found on him. Did you see his description? His name was Lucifer, from a word meaning "shining one." His brilliance was in his makeup, because every precious stone was his covering.

And the word sockets (v. 13) can also be translated pipes. Lucifer didn't play the organ; he was the organ. When he opened up his mouth, he was probably like a million-dollar organ. He was a blameless, flawless, perfect masterpiece.

Notice his place, along with his perfections. He was in Eden, the garden of God. Verse 14 says he was on the holy mountain of God, walking in the midst of the stones of fire. In other words, he was as close to God as he could possibly get.

Now, notice his position in verse 14:

> "You were the anointed cherub who covers, and I placed you there.
> You were on the holy mountain of God; you walked in the midst of
> the stones of fire."

He was a covering cherub. Now the cherubim are the honor guard of the angels. Their responsibility is to proclaim and protect the glory of God. They're at the top of God's angelic hierarchy.

By the abundance of your trade you were internally filled with violence and you sinned; therefore I have cast you as profane from the mountain of God. And I have destroyed you O covering cherub, from the midst of the stones of fire. Ezekiel 28:16

But Lucifer was not just a cherub. He was an anointed cherub. Of all the high-ranking cherubim, he was at the top of the list. He was the leader. He was in the highest position possible. There was no other angel higher than this shining one.

Then something changed. Something happened that would change the course of history.

> *"You were blameless in your ways from the day you were creat-*
> *ed, until unrighteousness was found in you. By the abundance of*
> *your trade you were internally filled with violence, and you sinned;*
> *therefore I have cast you as profane from the mountain of God.*
> *And I have destroyed you, O covering cherub, from the midst of the*
> *stones of fire. Your heart was lifted up because of your beauty; you*
> *corrupted your wisdom by reason of your splendor."*
>
> *Ezekiel 28:15-17*

> Rather than recognize his perfection as a gift from God, Lucifer allowed pride to well up inside of him.

He was perfect in every detail. But rather than recognize his perfection as a gift from God, he allowed pride to well up inside of him, when Lucifer allowed pride to enter his life, he forgot something. He forgot that he was just a creature.

What was the cause of rebellion? He forgot that those big diamonds didn't show up by themselves. He forgot that he didn't earn his position. He forgot that he didn't become a cherub because he woke up one day feeling "cherubby." He forgot that he was a created being, and he forgot his Creator.

Don't stand too long in front of a mirror, because eventually you're going to start looking good. You don't want to forget that you're a creature who has a Creator. Pride leads to self-worship, and self-worship is idolatry. If God has blessed you more this year than last year, you need to praise Him more. If you're praising Him less, you're on your way to becoming an idolater, because you're worshiping the benefit and not the Benefactor.

Some people find it hard to accept that a loving God would create the devil. In light of what you have seen in Ezekiel 28, how would you now respond to this argument?

_____

_____

_____

_____

_____

_____

_____

What place does pride have in your life? Are you proud in the sense that you're ungrateful to God for who you are, or have you become independent of Him because of who you are?

_____

_____

_____

_____

_____

_____

_____

Don't stand too long in front of a mirror, because eventually you're going to start looking good. You don't want to forget that you're a creature who has a Creator.

## 2. THE CONTENT OF SATAN'S REBELLION

The cause of Satan's rebellion was pride engendered by his own splendor. The content of his rebellion was simply negative volition: God created him with the ability to make decisions, and he chose to disobey God.

Satan's pride and willful disobedience are seen in five statements recorded in Isaiah 14. Each statement begins with "I will," which affirms that his focus was himself:

**1.** "*I will ascend to heaven.*" He already had access to heaven, so he wasn't just seeking a tour. He already had access to God; he was already moving in God's presence; and he was already on the mountain of God. So he's not talking about paying a visit; he's talking about ascendancy. In other words, he wanted to ascend with a view to occupying the throne.

**2.** "*I will raise my throne above the stars of God.*" Job 38:7 refers to angels as morning stars, so what Satan was saying was that he wanted to rule over all the angels. Though he was the chief cherub, he was only in charge of what God allowed him to be in charge of. He was a sort of go-between for God and the other angels. And a third of the angels joined him (Revelation 12:4).

**3**. "*I will sit on the mount of assembly in the recesses of the north.*" Psalm 48:2 says that the center of God's kingdom rule, where He con-

Satan's pride and willful disobedience are seen in five statements recorded in Isaiah 14. Each statement begins with "I will," which affirms that his focus was himself.

trols the affairs of the universe, is in the far north. In other words, Satan didn't want to pray, "Thy kingdom come, Thy will be done," but "My kingdom come, my will be done." Everybody prays one of two prayers. Everybody promotes one of two kingdoms.

Everybody lives for one of two gods. Satan wanted to usurp God's throne. Don't live your life like he succeeded, because he didn't.

> Satan can't stand to be around us when we're worshiping because we are giving to God what he so desperately wants for himself.

**4.** "*I will ascend above the heights of the clouds.*" In the Old Testament, clouds were associated with the glory of the Lord (see Exodus 16:10 and 40:34). He wanted glory. He wanted praise. He wanted worship. Remember what he offered Jesus when he was tempting our Lord? And he said to Him, 'All these things will I give You, if You fall down and worship me' (Matthew 4:9).

Satan's desire to be worshiped is the reason he cannot hang around when we are worshiping God. He can't stand to be around us when we are worshiping, because we are giving to God what he so desperately wants for himself. Not only that, but when we worship God he is reminded of his old job description and the job he'll never get to do again.

God does not share the glory that only He deserves.

> "*I am the Lord, that is My name. I will not give My glory to another, nor My praise to graven images.*"
>
> *Isaiah 42:8*

**5.** *"I will make myself like the Most High."* That's an interesting statement, because it's the statement of a fool. This is a creature looking up to God, who is omnipotent, omnipresent, omniscient, omni-everything, and this fool says "I want to be like Him." To be like Him would mean there would be two Gods. That's impossible, or God wouldn't be God.

Satan was probably referring more to what God has, and he was probably focusing primarily on His independence. God is accountable to no one outside of Himself. And jealous Satan wants that—total independence and freedom.

> Satan's sin was so grievous because he was never tempted by anyone outside of himself. There was nobody around to tempt him. He came up with his plan of rebellion all by himself.

Satan's sin was so grievous because he was never tempted by anyone outside of himself. There was nobody around to tempt him. He came up with his plan of rebellion all by himself. He had intellect, he had opportunity, he had service, and he had fellowship. But he didn't realize that when you don't do it God's way, it doesn't work.

**You too, have a choice to follow God or to rebel against Him. Think about the life choices you have made for yourself. Are you walking in obedience or disobedience to your Creator?**

_____

_____

_____

_____

---

---

---

---

**Look back at Satan's five "I will" statements. Do any of them sound familiar to you? If you have coveted something that does not belong to you, then ask God right now to forgive you and to help you walk in obedience to Him.**

---

---

---

---

---

---

---

# 3. THE CURSE OF SATAN'S REBELLION

Satan became proud and rebelled against God, but he forgot something: We can always control our decisions, but we cannot control the consequences. We can devise a plan of rebellion, and we can carry it out, but only God controls the consequences of our decisions.

What were Satan's consequences? He was "cut down to the earth" and will be "thrust down to Sheol, to the recesses of the pit" (Isaiah 14:12, 15). He lost his position and privilege, his character was corrupted, and his power was perverted.

When this angelic conflict finally comes to its conclusion and Satan makes his last move (depending on God's calendar, not Satan's), Lucifer will reach his final destination. But it won't be above the heights of the clouds:

> Satan became proud and rebelled against God, but he forgot something: We can always control our decisions, but we cannot control the consequences.

*"And the devil who deceived them was thrown into the lake of fire and brimstone, where the beast and the false prophet are also; and they will be tormented day and night forever and ever."*

*Revelation 20:10*

Hell is a sort of holding cell, but there's a boiling pot called the lake of fire. It's a place of torment, and it's Satan's final home. It's where he will spend eternity. After Satan's rebellion, God created this place just for him and his angels. The lake of fire was never intended for man or woman, but many men and women will go there because they chose to let Satan be their god. Actually, the lake of fire is the answer to the sinner's prayer.

That consequence is permanent, because there are no second chances for the devil and his angels (Hebrews 2:16).

> *"There is only one true God, and He alone deserves all the glory, honor, and praise. He will spare nothing to preserve His glory. We must recognize who He is, humble ourselves before Him, and worship Him."*

King Nebuchadnezzar was proud at one time, but God caused him to stop and look up. Do you know what the king said after acknowledging God as God?

> *"But at the end of that period I, Nebuchadnezzar, raised my eyes toward heaven, and my reason returned to me, and I blessed the Most High and praised and honored Him who lives forever; for His dominion is an everlasting dominion, and His kingdom endures from generation to generation. And all the inhabitants of the earth*

*are accounted as nothing, but He does according to His will in the host of heaven and among the inhabitants of earth; and no one can ward off His hand or say to Him, "What hast Thou done?"... Now I Nebuchadnezzar praise, exalt, and honor the King of heaven, for all His works are true and His ways just, and He is able to humble those who walk in pride."*

*Daniel 4:34-35,37*

King Nebuchadnezzar was proud at one time, but God caused him to stop and look up.

**If you are not living in obedience to the Lord Jesus Christ, then you're living in obedience to an angel that was thrown out of heaven. Will you repent and make Jesus your Lord?  Maybe Jesus is Lord of your life, but you have been living in rebellion without realizing the seriousness of your actions. Read I John 1:9 and make it your prayer.**

# NOTES

# LESSON 10

## THE CHARACTER OF SATAN

*Satan...* *wasn't always ugly. Created in perfection, he was the archangel, the anointed cherub, and the worship leader. But watching God receive all the glory was a little too much for him, because he wanted that glory for himself.*

God will not share His glory with anyone, so the anointed cherub was out of luck. He became jealous, and from that jealousy developed a burning hatred for God. Satan hates God for keeping all of His glory to Himself.

> Because he was unable to deny God glory, he set himself on a program to divert glory from God. He planned to accomplish this by getting other angels to try to divert God's glory to him.

Because he was unable to deny God glory, he set himself on a program to divert glory from God. He planned to accomplish this by getting other angels to try to divert God's glory to him.

Satan's sentence was severe because his curse was given with no possibility of parole.

His efforts resulted in the greatest feud in history, the mother of all wars, when God's creation began a revolt against Him. That revolt led to the angelic conflict, the battle in heavenly places, in which we are now involved.

We have looked at Lucifer's beginning and his rebellion, but now it's time to turn to his character after the Fall. Remember, if you're going to fight intelligently, you need to understand who it is you're fighting.

# 1. THE CURSE OF SATAN'S CHARACTER

When he was living in heaven among all the other angels, Satan's name was Lucifer. The word meant "shining one." If the angels were like stars, then you might think of Lucifer as being like the sun. But he became prideful and decided that he would become like the Most High God. Lucifer decided to rebel against God and God cast him out of heaven.

In Luke 10:18, Jesus referred to this point in time when Lucifer was cast out of heaven: "And He said to them, 'I was watching Satan fall from heaven like lightning.'" Now, what was his name when he was living in heaven? Lucifer. And what is the name Jesus uses here? Satan.

So Lucifer got a name change before he got the boot. Jesus watched Satan, not Lucifer, fall from heaven. God changed his name from Lucifer ("shining one") to Satan ("adversary, opposer"). In the Bible, names are very important because they reflect a person's character. And just as the names of God reflect God's character, the names of the devil reflect the devil's character.

Also notice in this verse that Jesus said He was watching when Satan fell from heaven. Do you realize that Jesus had not been born at that time? He's saying that He was there, but how? John 1:1 tells us how: "In the beginning was the Word, and the Word was with God, and the Word was God." Jesus Christ is God, and He was telling His disciples about His pre-existence.

Now Lucifer got a name change and was booted out of heaven. He fell like lightning, so it all happened pretty quickly. But the curse of his character got worse. Not only did he lose his previous home, but he has been given a new one. God handed down a severe sentence in response to his rebellion. This is a severe sentence because this curse allows no possibility of parole. God did not make provision for the fallen angels; He only made provision for fallen man.

> "For assuredly He does not give help to angels, but He gives help to the descendants of Abraham. Therefore, He had to be made like His brethren in all things, that He might become a merciful and faithful high priest in things pertaining to God, to make propitiation for the sins of the people."
>
> Hebrews 2:16-17

Satan wasn't tricked, he plotted his rebellion with full light. And because of his rebellious character, he was given a curse without a remedy.

Why was no provision made for Satan? Because he sinned with too much light. He was not enticed into sin like we are. He wasn't born into sin like we are. He was perfect in every detail. He had insights into God that we will not have until we reach heaven. He lived in the very presence of God. He knew what he was doing. He wasn't tricked. He plotted his rebellion with full light. And because of his rebellious character, he was given a curse without a remedy.

In the Bible, a person's name often reflects his character. When we accept Jesus Christ as our Savior and Lord, we are called Christians (followers of Christ). Does your life give an accurate picture of the character of Jesus Christ to those who are watching?

_____

_____

_____

_____

_____

_____

_____

Some people refuse to accept a loving God who would send people to hell and the lake of fire. Based on what you have studied, how could you reason with such a person by using the Scripture?

_____

_____

_____

_____

_____

_____

_____

## 2. THE CONTENT OF SATAN'S CHARACTER

The Word of God gives several different names to the devil. Understanding the meanings of these names will provide much insight into his character.

> "And a great sign appeared in heaven: a woman clothed with the sun, and the moon under her feet, and on her head a crown of twelve stars; and she was with child; and she cried out, being in labor and in

*pain to give birth. And another sign appeared in heaven and behold a red dragon having seven heads and ten horns, and on his heads were seven diadems. And his tail swept away a third of the stars of heaven, and threw them to the earth. And the dragon stood before the woman who was about to give birth, so that when she gave birth he might devour her child...And there was war in heaven, Michael and his angels waging war with the dragon. And the dragon and his angels waged war, and they were not strong enough, and there was no longer a place found for them in heaven. And the great dragon was thrown down, the serpent of old who is called the devil and Satan, who deceives the whole world; he was thrown down to the earth, and his angels were thrown down with him."*

*Revelation 12:1-4, 7-9*

A number of names are given for Satan in this passage. One name given in verse 3 is dragon. In fact, verse 3 calls him a great red dragon. Verse 4 calls him the dragon. Verse 7, again, calls him the dragon. And in verse 9, he is referred to as the serpent of old. A dragon is basically a serpent on steroids, so he is a destructive being.

> The Word of God gives several different names to the devil. Understanding the meanings of these names will provide much insight into his character.

Satan is also a destroyer. John 10:10 says, "The thief comes only to steal, and kill, and destroy; I came that they might have life, and might have it abundantly."

The devil can give you money, power, prestige, friends, and fun, but it's all a trick. He will deceive you so that he can steal from you, kill you, and destroy you.

Look at the scope of his destructive power:

*"We know that no one who is born of God sins; but He who was born of God keeps him, and the evil one does not touch him. We know that we are of God, and the whole world lies in the power of the evil one."*

*1 John 5:18-19*

> The devil can give you money, power, prestige, friends, and fun, but it's all a trick. Then he will deceive you so that he can steal from you, kill you, and destroy you.

Did you get that? The whole world. In other words, this world has been adequately demonized. It sits in his hands.

He is also called the god of this world (2 Corinthians 4:4) and the prince of the power of the air (Ephesians 2:2). He seeks to bring destruction into every aspect of life. John recorded Jesus' description of Satan in John 8:44. Look at what Jesus said:

*"You are of your father the devil, and you want to do the desires of your father. He was a murderer from the beginning, and does not stand in the truth, because there is no truth in him. Whenever he speaks a lie, he speaks from his own nature; for he is a liar, and the father of lies."*

Whenever he speaks, he lies. He speaks from his own nature, for he is a liar and the father of lies. Satan makes promises that he will not keep, or sometimes he'll make promises without telling us the whole story. Then, when his promises are delivered, they're nothing like you thought you were getting.

The content of his character is also clear from another name, and that is devil. This is a very important word in understanding Satan because the word devil means "accuser or slanderer." He wants to injure the reputation of God so that God will not get glory, and he wants to injure the reputation of God's people so that God's name can be maligned.

The world and the universe operate like a court. Everything happens in a legal type of setting. Throughout Scripture, we see God bringing a charge against people. Satan was brought into court, charged with rebellion, and found guilty. His sentence was the lake of fire. He is now like a prisoner on death row.

So when the Bible calls him the devil, God is not trying to conjure up in our heads a picture of an ugly-looking guy with horns, a red jumpsuit, and a pitchfork. He wants us to understand the character of this opposer. When the word devil is used, God is making a point about that aspect of his character. When the word Satan is used, God is making a point about that aspect of his character. When the term father of lies is used, God is making a point about that aspect of his character.

An example of this is found in Ephesians 4:26-27, where it says, "Be angry, and yet do not sin; do not let the sun go down on your anger, and do not give the devil an opportunity." Why the devil? Why not say the evil one or the dragon or the serpent? Because the devil is the accuser. And he accuses us before God.

> *"And I heard a loud voice in heaven, saying, 'Now the salvation, and the power, and the kingdom of our God and the authority of His Christ have come, for the accuser of our brethren has been thrown down, who accuses them before our God day and night."*
> *Revelation 12:10*

This devilish activity of accusing is very important to Satan. He has been in God's court before, and he knows what kind of judge God is. God is righteous and perfect, and therefore must deal with sin. So the devil delights in running to Him with information about our sins.

When we sin, we are not in fellowship with God. Satan wants to accuse us so that our fellowship will be broken and he will have the freedom to operate in our lives.

When we sin, we are not in fellowship with God. Satan wants to accuse us so that our fellowship will be broken and he will have the freedom to operate in our lives, either directly or through his demonic host. We are not to give him that opportunity, but we are to resist him (James 4:7; 1 Peter 5:9).

**Another name for the devil is the father of lies. Every lie that has ever been told has originated from him. Has Satan influenced you through any lies or half-truths you tell?**

_____

_____

_____

_____

_____

_____

_____

_____

_____

**John 8:44 says that Satan was a murderer from the beginning. Read Genesis 2:17; 3:4; 4:7-8, 23. What pattern do you see?**

_____

_____

_____

---
---
---
---
---
---

## 3. THE CONQUEST OF SATAN'S CHARACTER

How do we avoid letting him win? How do we deny him an opportunity in our lives? The solution is in Revelation 12:11:

*"And they overcame him because of the blood of the Lamb and because of the word of their testimony, and they did not love their life even to death."*

You need three things in order to keep the devil from ruining you: the cross, confession, and commitment. Of first importance is the cross. John mentions "the blood of the Lamb." The blood is a reference to the death of Christ on the cross. His death rendered Satan powerless.

Satan was judged by the death of Christ, and we receive help through the blood of Christ. Romans 8:31-32 says, "What then shall we say to these things? If God is for us, who is against us? He who did not spare His own Son, but delivered Him up for us all, how will He not also with Him freely give us all things?"

Confession, or the word of testimony, also contributes to the conquest of Satan's character. Your testimony says you belong to Jesus Christ.

If you know Christ, then, because of His death, you have a lot of freebies to pick up.

> Of first importance is the cross. Christ's death rendered Satan powerless.

Jesus Christ is on your side, and He is the One who justifies, He is the One who died, He is the One who was raised, He is the One who is at the right hand of God, and He is the One who also intercedes for us (Romans 8:33-34).

Jesus serves as our attorney, or our advocate. And every time Satan accuses us, Jesus stands up to say, "That has already been taken care of. I paid for that."

The reason Satan keeps accusing and accusing and accusing is that he wants us to forget to confess (1 John 1:9). If we forget to confess, he can get a foot in the door of our lives.

Confession, or the word of testimony, also contributes to the conquest of Satan's character. Your testimony says you belong to Jesus Christ. It has to do with how you speak and how you live, and whether you are adequately and accurately reflecting who Jesus is. If you're not reflecting Him accurately, or if you're ashamed for other people to know you're a Christian, then you have no power over the devil.

Finally, our commitment will defeat Satan. When we do not love our lives even to death, Satan will not be able to accuse us.

**Have you confessed Him as Savior and Lord? Or are you ashamed of Him? If you are professing Jesus as Lord in private but not in public, ask yourself why.**

_____

_____

_____

_____

_____

_____

**Have you committed yourself to following Christ, even if it means losing your life? Are you willing to stand for Jesus Christ, no matter the cost?**

_____

_____

_____

_____

_____

_____

_____

Confession, or the word of testimony, also contributes to the conquest of Satan's character. Your testimony says you belong to Jesus Christ.

The Emancipation Proclamation, signed in 1863, freed America's slaves. However, even though someone says on a piece of paper, "You're free," you can still think like a slave and act like a slave if you have not experienced what's on paper.

When you come to Jesus Christ, He sets you free. Wouldn't it be sad for Jesus to set you free only for you to keep obeying the devil, following the devil, living for the devil, obeying the devil, and coming under the control of the devil?

As you learn to depend on the blood of Christ, you'll be able to praise Him, saying, "Yes, thank God Almighty, I really am free at last!"

# THE STRATEGY OF SATAN

*The farmer...* was tired of having his melons stolen by thieves, so he decided to do something about it. He spent so much time cultivating the melons that he couldn't let the thieves continue.

His idea was brilliant. He put up a sign that read, "One of these melons is poisoned." The next day, he went out to check his melons, and not one of them was missing. He was quite satisfied with himself for tricking the thief.

## " There's no fooling the devil. "

Two days later, he went to check on the melons and noticed that someone had tampered with his sign. The sign now read, "Two of these melons are poisoned. "The farmer lost his whole crop because he didn't know which melon was poisoned.

There's no fooling the devil. It doesn't matter what you come up with; he can always come up with something better. No matter what resolutions you come up with, he can always change the sign. No matter what strategy you come up with, you cannot compete with Satan. He is the master deceiver, and your only hope for survival is to know the strategy of his deception.

# 1. THE POWER OF SATAN'S DECEPTION

Put Satan's power up against the power of our omnipotent God, and there's no contest. Satan cannot "out-power" God. So he has developed a strategy of deception to capture the attention of those who are not spiritually attuned.

> *"Let no one in any way deceive you, for [the day of the Lord] will not come unless the apostasy comes first, and the man of lawlessness is revealed, the son of destruction, who opposes and exalts himself above every so-called god or object of worship, so that he takes his seat in the temple of God, displaying himself as being God"*
>
> 2 Thessalonians 2:3-4

These verses refer to the time when the Antichrist, empowered by Satan, will deceive the world.

> *"Then that lawless one will be revealed whom the Lord will slay with the breath of His mouth and bring to an end by the appearance of His coming; that is, the one whose coming is in accord with the activity of Satan, with all power and signs and false wonders, and with all the deception of wickedness for those who perish, because they did not receive the love of the truth so as to be saved."*
>
> 2 Thessalonians 2:8-10

Satan has to maneuver what is, because he cannot create what is not. Because he does not have the power of creation, he has to maximize the performance of deception. He has turned deception into an art form. Second Thessalonians says that his deception through the lawless one will be so powerful that he will sit in the temple and cause people to think that he is God.

Don't deceive yourself and say, "Not me. It'll never happen." Two factors explain Satan's mastery of deception. First, he has constitutional superiority over men and women in that he is an angel, a spirit being, without the limitations of flesh and blood. That's why it is impossible to compete on his level of deception.

Second, he has years of experience. You are not the first human he has come up against. He is a master chameleon, and he can become any color he needs in order to make his point.

Another reason for his power is that he has a massive organization working for him. If you were asked to give an address to the Mafia, you wouldn't be able to do it. The Mafia has camouflaged itself in the midst of legitimate businesses. Members of the Mafia go to work wearing suits and ties and carrying briefcases, infiltrating organizations and disguising themselves. Satan and his demons work the same way.

This is why there is no substitute for Bible doctrine. You should enjoy choir, fellowship, and worship, but none of that can replace Bible doctrine in your life. Bible doctrine gives you the meat and potatoes of the Christian life.

Doctrine serves as a filter for the soul in order to catch false teaching that will try to infiltrate your life. When your life is filled with doctrine, and when you understand the categories of truth in the Word of God, you may not know all the details, but you'll know when something is not right.

> Doctrine serves as a filter for the soul in order to catch false teaching that will try to infiltrate your life.

Matthew 13:19 says that when people hear the Word but cannot understand it, Satan comes along and snatches the Word. He knows that if the Word of God sticks to our spiritual bones, he will not have room to maneuver.

Read Ephesians 2:4-6. How does Satan's power compare to that of God's?

_____

_____

_____

_____

_____

_____

_____

How much doctrine do you know?

_____

_____

_____

_____

_____

_____

Read Hebrews 5:11-14. Are you still feeding on milk, or are you ready for solid food?

_____

_____

_____

_____

_____

_____

_____

## 2. THE PROGRAM OF SATAN'S DECEPTION

Satan's plan is to be such a wonderful counterfeit that he leads people astray. His program of deception hasn't changed since his encounter with Eve in Genesis 3. Let's review some of the things he told Eve.

First of all, he told her, "You can be like God." The thought of becoming like the Most High had appealed to Satan, so he decided to try it on Eve, too. He was telling her to set up her own kingdom and take matters into her own hands. He wanted Eve to buy the lie that she would be autonomous, that she would be independent, and that she would not have to answer to God anymore.

Then he told her, "You will know good and evil." In other words, he was saying, "You can make your own decisions about right and wrong. You don't need God telling you what to do." A church member once said, "I'm never going to come to Oak Cliff Bible Fellowship." When asked why, he said, "I want sermons that make me feel good. I don't need anybody telling me what to do." That is exactly what Satan told Eve.

> Satan's plan is to be such a wonderful counterfeit that he leads people astray. His program of deception hasn't changed since his encounter with Eve in Genesis 3.

Notice what else he told her. He said, "You won't die." He was presenting a situation in which there would be no consequences for her actions. And then he said to her, "Your eyes will be opened." He was saying to her that personal pleasure would become more important than objective truth. Satan cannot stand objective truth. He does not want us to believe something simply because God said it, whether we have experienced it or not. He has all kinds of systems in place to deceive us from objective, stated truth.

One of the things he wants us to believe is that truth is ever changing. This philosophy, known as relativism, has behind it the idea that what's true today may not be tomorrow.

Or he wants us to believe that truth is merely personal, which is subjectivism. That is it may be true for one person, but it's not true for another. Because Satan cannot stand objective truth, he works in the counterfeit business. He uses counterfeit doctrine (1 Timothy 4:1) and counterfeit miracles. He offers a counterfeit communion table (1 Corinthians 10:20¬21), counterfeit spirituality (Galatians 3:2-3), and a counterfeit gospel (Galatians 1:11-12).

Satan cannot stand objective truth. He does not want us to believe something simply because God said it, whether we have experienced it or not.

Paul also warns of counterfeit teachers, saying in 2 Corinthians 11:13-14 that "such men are false apostles, deceitful workers, disguising themselves as apostles of Christ. And no wonder, for even Satan disguises himself as an angel of light."

**Do you believe that truth is absolute? Read John 1:14, 17; 8:32; 14:6; 16:13; and 17:17, and note what John says about truth.**

_____

_____

_____

_____

_____

_____

**Can you think of ways Satan uses counterfeit doctrine, miracles, and teachers today? What is the real test of truth?**

_____

_____

_____

_____

_____

_____

_____

# 3. THE PROCESS OF SATAN'S DECEPTION

Satan's deceptive strategy is a process that involves four stages. James gives us insight into how this process works:

> "Let no one say when he is tempted, "I am being tempted by God"; for God cannot be tempted by evil, and He Himself does not tempt anyone. But each one is tempted when he is carried away and enticed by his own lust. Then when lust has conceived, it gives birth to sin; and when sin is accomplished, it brings forth death."
>
> James 1:13-15

The first stage starts with desire, or lust. Desire for something is not necessarily bad. The problem comes in the illegitimate application of a legitimate desire. And that is one definition of temptation—an attempt to get you to do a good thing in a bad way.

> Desire for something is not necessarily bad. The problem comes in the illegitimate application of a legitimate desire.

Desire for food is good, but gluttony is sin. Sexual desire is good, but immorality is sin. A desire to sleep is fine, but lying in bed all day and being lazy is sin.

> Remember what Jesus did when He was confronted by the devil? He dealt with it right then and there.

Satan knows we cannot skip the desires because they were given by God, so he wants to control how those desires are used. The application is the issue in temptation. Satan wants our desires to be master instead of us being master over our desires.

Second, desire leads to deception. James says we can be carried away and enticed by our own lust. The idea is that of a fisherman throwing his baited hook into the water. Satan plants an evil thought or idea in our minds by taking something legitimate and then planting an evil thought next to it in order to effect the illegitimate application of a legitimate desire. This is how he worked through David in 1 Chronicles 21. He gave David the thought of numbering the people, and then David got the idea that he didn't need God because of the size of his army. Because of the illegitimate application of a legitimate desire, 70,000 people died.

Satan caused Ananias and Sapphira to lie to Peter about the money they were giving in Acts. What happened? They died. Satan planted the thought of betraying Jesus into Judas' mind. How did it end? Judas committed suicide.

Once desire has led to deception, the next step is disobedience. When lust has conceived, it gives birth to sin (James 1:15). So when the desire is applied illegitimately, it is then sin. The desire is not sin, but the illegitimate application of that desire is sin. For example, if you're single and have sexual desires, you are not sinning. But when you apply those desires illegitimately, you have entered into sin.

And, finally, when a desire has been applied illegitimately, sin is born; and sin brings forth death. This death comes because we have missed the goodness of God and we have broken our fellowship with Him.

Remember what Jesus did when He was confronted by the devil? He didn't sleep on it. He didn't say, "Let Me think about it and get back to you later." He dealt with it right then and there.

**Isn't it freeing to understand that our desires are only sinful when we act on them illegitimately? But how do you kill your desires before they take you down that road to deception, disobedience, and death? Read 2 Corinthians 10:5 before answering.**

_____

_____

_____

_____

_____

_____

_____

**Think about a specific sin you struggle with, and ask God to show you a practical way you can "take every thought captive" before being led into sin.**

_____

_____

_____

_____

_____

_____

## 4. THE PURPOSE OF SATAN'S DECEPTION

The ultimate purpose of Satan's deceptive strategy is to defect us form the will of God. He wants to interrupt God from getting the glory, and he wants to stop non-believers from getting saved (2 Corinthians 4:3-4) because the more people get saved, the more glory God gets. So he doesn't want believers witnessing to their lost friends.

He wants to keep us ineffective. That's why he is keeping so many people depressed, discouraged, and under their circumstances. He want to keep us under there because he knows we can do nothing for God if we're miserable. So he'll make life miserable, circumstances miserable, and families too miserable, because God won't get glory if we're too miserable to give it to Him. In fact, he will twist situations so that we will begin to blame God for our misery. That means we're not only not giving God glory, but we're taking joy away from Him. Satan will cause us to blame God for things that are Satan's fault because Satan himself is the master deceiver.

Satan also wants to frustrate God's will for our lives. Jesus said, "Get behind Me, Satan!" to Peter in Matthew 16:23 because Satan had influenced Peter's thinking.

Satan may be giving you a tough time, and you may have to go through even more hard times to follow Christ. But when you finish the race and stand on that winner's block, and when that gold crown is placed on your head, you'll be able to say, "It was worth it. It was worth it."

Jesus Christ's death left Satan powerless. That devil may have the power to deceive, to make you think that he's more than he really is, but you know the truth.

Satan is keeping so many people depressed, discouraged, and under their circumstances. He wants to keep us under there because he knows we can do nothing for God if we're miserable.

Jesus Christ's death left Satan powerless. That devil may have the power to deceive, to make you think that he's more than he really is, but you know the truth. Don't fall for his tricks.

**Satan wants to interrupt your praise of God, and he wants to divert God's glory. Read 1 Thessalonians 5:16-18 and consider how you can walk in constant worship.**

_____

_____

_____

_____

_____

_____

**How is it possible to determine God's will for your life when Satan wants to frustrate and confuse you? Read Romans 12:1-2.**

_____

_____

_____

_____

_____

_____

_____

# NOTES

# THE DEFEAT
# OF SATAN

*Have you ever...* made a decision that turned out to be an even bigger decision than you expected when you made it? Did you feel involved in something that was over your head, beyond your capacity to deal with?

Satan experienced this problem when he got in over his head. When he decided to rebel he didn't know that he would spin a set of circumstances that would cost him eternity. He thought his gamble would win, evidently believing he had the power to pull enough weight to be able to rival God and win.

> Little did he know that his gamble to rebel would be defeated the moment after he decided to do it.

The moment of Satan's rebellion was in fact, the moment of his defeat, all because Satan overestimated himself and underestimated God.

## 1. SATAN WAS DEFEATED STRATEGICALLY

Satan rebelled and his strategy failed. It was a strategic defeat. He was defeated the moment he sinned because he was a creature rebelling against a

Creator on whom he depended for his existence as a creature. So whenever we consider the devil, we must never consider him without a proper view of the Lord. If you look at him without a picture of God, then you will be looking at an optical illusion.

When the creature rebelled against the Creator, God decided to allow the rebellion, but then use that rebellion as a way of accomplishing His plan. In allowing Satan's rebellion, God created opportunity to bring more glory to Himself. He told Satan to try His servant Job because He knew Job would bring Him more glory than if the rebellion and test had not come.

If God allows Satan to test you, you must not focus on the test or what Satan is doing.

> If God allows Satan to test you, you must not focus on the test or what Satan is doing. You don't want the devil to block you from seeing God at work in your life.

You don't want the devil to block you from seeing God at work in your life. It's an opportunity to say, like Job, "Though He slay me, I will hope in Him" (Job 13:15). It's an opportunity to say, like Job, "Shall we indeed accept good from God and not accept adversity?" (Job 2:10). It's an opportunity to say, like Job, "The Lord gave and the Lord has taken away. Blessed be the name of the Lord" (Job 1:21). If you haven't said that because of the size of your trial, then the trial is having more power over you than God wants it to have.

Peter had to face a trial of the devil, but look at what he says in 1 Peter 1:6:

*"In this you greatly rejoice, even though now for a little while, if necessary, you have been distressed by various trials, that the proof of*

*your faith, being more precious than gold which is perishable, even though tested by fire, may be found to result in praise and glory and honor at the revelation of Jesus Christ."*

Then, in 4:19, he says, "Therefore, let those also who suffer according to the will of God entrust their souls to a faithful Creator in doing what is right."

If you're in a trial, praise Him — not for the pain or the inconvenience, but for the opportunity to bring more glory to Him. He wants us to have a divine viewpoint. An example of this is found in 2 Corinthians 12, where Paul was given a "thorn in the flesh." The Bible never specifically says what that "thorn" was, but it was causing Paul great pain, anguish, and consternation.

*"And because of the surpassing greatness of the revelations, for this reason, to keep me from exalting myself, there was given me a thorn in the flesh, a messenger of Satan to buffet me — to keep me from exalting myself. Concerning this I entreated the Lord three times that it might depart from me. And He has said to me, "My grace is sufficient for you, for My power is perfected in weakness." Most gladly, therefore, I will rather boast about my weaknesses, that the power of Christ may dwell in me."*

*2 Corinthians 12:7-9*

Paul evidently struggled with pride. He was a proud man before he got saved, and that pride must have moved over into his Christian experience. And now he had even more to be proud of, because God had raised him up to a prominent place in Christianity. He had received more revelation than the other apostles; he was going to write more books of the Bible than the other apostles; and he was the only apostle who got to go to heaven and come back to talk about it. He was uniquely blessed, and pride was something he had to battle with.

God assisted Paul with his struggle by allowing Satan to bring something into Paul's life that was too much for him to handle. Paul had cried out to God three times for help. Then God basically told Paul, "I'm not going to take you out of this trial, but I'll join you in the trial."

If Paul had looked at the devil, he would have said, "The devil is messing with me." But, because he had heard from God, he knew that God was using Satan's "thorn" to humble Paul so that God could use him in ministry.

> God assisted Paul with his struggle by allowing Satan to bring something into Paul's life that was too much for him to handle.

This principle is also true in the life of Peter. Luke 11 shows Peter as prideful and independent, and God hates pride more than anything else because it reminds Him of the rebellion of the devil. If you're a proud person—in your thoughts, your talk, or your walk—then you're in trouble, because God will keep you humble. He will force you to depend on Him, and He will not allow independence to rise up in your life.

*"Simon, Simon, behold, Satan has demanded permission to sift you like wheat; but I have prayed for you, that your faith may not fail; and you, when once you have turned again, strengthen your brothers."*

Luke 22:31-32

Satan demanded what? Permission. So, before he can mess with you, he has to get God's approval before he can attempt to make your life miserable. If you're walking with God and life is miserable, don't look at Satan. Look at God and ask, "God, why did You give him permission?" In other words, go to God. Satan wants to keep your eyes off of God.

Another way God uses Satan is to judge His children. Saul had rebelled against God and become independent. Watch how God responded: "Now the Spirit of the LORD departed from Saul, and an evil spirit from the Lord terrorized him" (1 Samuel 16:14).

> "Now it came about on the next day that an evil spirit from God came mightily upon Saul, and he raved in the midst of the house, while David was playing the harp with his hand, as usual; and a spear was in Saul's hand. And Saul hurled the spear for he thought, "I will pin David to the wall." But David escaped from his presence twice. Now Saul was afraid of David, for the Lord was with him but had departed from Saul."
>
> 1 Samuel 18:10-12

God will allow evil to do its work in your life. He will give evil spirits permission to make your life miserable if you, like Saul, are living in rebellion. Just remember that nothing happens outside of the sovereign control of God. Don't put your eyes on the devil, because he's not going to help you beat the situation.

Nothing happens outside of the sovereign control of God. Don't put your eyes on the devil, because he's not going to help you beat the situation.

**How have you seen God's will accomplished through the lives of ungodly men? Read Habakkuk 1:1-11. How has God used evil men in the past to accomplish His purposes?**

_____

_____

_____

_____

_____

_____

_____

**In what ways has God allowed your circumstances, though ugly on the outside, to benefit you in your relationship with Him?**

_____

_____

_____

_____

_____

_____

## 2. SATAN WAS DEFEATED PROPHETICALLY

Not only was Satan defeated strategically, but he was defeated prophetically through the Word of God in Genesis 3:15: "And I will put enmity between you and the woman, and between your seed and her seed; he shall bruise you on the head, and you shall bruise him on the heel."

First, notice what God said to the serpent "I will." Do you remember our study of Isaiah 14 when Lucifer made five "I will" statements? This is the beginning of a battle of wills, a conflict of whose will is greater.

Not only was Satan defeated strategically, but he was- defeated prophetically through the Word of God.

The serpent, or Satan, is to be bruised by a human being—the seed of the woman. So a man would have to be the one to bruise the devil. Also, suffering is to be involved. The serpent would bruise His heel, but He would crush the serpent's head.

> Even when it looks like the devil has won, there's always a Seth. There's always a Noah.

Satan knew that the woman's seed was going to crush him. Eve had two sons—Cain and Abel. Abel followed God. So when Satan saw Abel bringing God offerings that God accepted, he decided he needed to get rid of that seed. Satan probably believed that Abel was the promised seed so he got Cain to kill Abel.

What Satan didn't count on was what happened in Genesis 4:25:

> *"And Adam had relations with his wife again; and she gave birth to a son and named him Seth, for, she said, God has appointed me another offspring in place of Abel; for Cain killed him."*

But what does this have to do with the angelic conflict? Verse 26 says, "And to Seth, to him also a son was born; and he called his name Enosh. Then men began to call upon the name of the Lord." God always has somebody else or some other plan to make what He plans to always come true.

Satan was thrown a curve ball, so he reached further in Genesis 6. The sons of God and the daughters of men committed sexual immorality, and Satan was sure he would be able to corrupt all mankind. But look at verse 8:

"But Noah found favor in the eyes of the Lord."

Think about the word *seed* in Genesis 3:15. Biologically speaking, women do not have seed; only men do. To whom does this verse point? Compare your answer with Luke 1:34-35.

_____

_____

_____

_____

_____

_____

_____

God has promised Satan's defeat. Read Isaiah 14:24, 27, then record what you learn about the faithfulness of God's promises.

_____

_____

_____

_____

_____

_____

_____

## 3. SATAN WAS DEFEATED SPIRITUALLY

Satan has been defeated strategically and prophetically, but an even bigger disappointment to him is his spiritual defeat. The cross of Jesus Christ was the ultimate curve ball. "Now judgment is upon this world; now the ruler of this world shall be cast out. And I, if I be lifted up from the earth, will draw all men to Myself." (John 12:31-32).

Satan has been judged by what Jesus Christ did on the cross (John 16:11), because the cross removed the curse of sin. Satan has experienced living under the curse of God, and he wants us to experience it, too. But Jesus, while on that cross, removed the curse from us.

Galatians 3:13 says Christ redeemed us from the curse of the Law. There was a curse there because the Law's very purpose was to show us that we could not keep it. Therefore, it exposed to us our sins. The good news is that Jesus removed that curse and, at the same time, judged Satan so completely. Read Hebrews 10:12-14:

> Satan has experienced living under the curse of God, and he wants us to experience it too. But Jesus, while on that cross, removed the curse from us.

*"But He, having offered one sacrifice for sins for all time, sat down at the right hand of God, waiting from that time onward until His enemies be made a footstool for His feet. For by one offering He has perfected for all time those who are sanctified."*

As Christians, we don't have to worry about whether we'll be put back under the curse if we sin one year from now. When He died, He did not just die for the sins we did and are doing, but He even paid for the sins we haven't done yet. He has us covered forever.

**Does death scare you? Satan wants you to be afraid, but if you're a Christian, you can take comfort in God's Word. Read 2 Corinthians 5:8 and Hebrews 2:14-15. What do these verses say about the death of the Christian?**

_____

_____

_____

_____

_____

_____

_____

## 4. SATAN WAS DEFEATED ETERNALLY

The biggest blow to Satan was the magnitude of his defeat. It is a defeat that will last for all eternity. Though he will forever be the loser in the angelic conflict, his defeat came about in stages.

The moment Lucifer sinned, he was stripped of his name and booted out of heaven (Ezekiel 28). He still had access to God's presence; he could pay a visit, but could no longer live there.

Still to come is a thousand-year period where the devil will be confined and unable to touch anyone (Revelation 20:1-3). During this time, Jesus Christ will set up His kingdom on earth. He will rule for 1,000 years without any satanic interference, because Satan will be locked up. Then, after the thousand-year period is up, the devil will be "thrown into the lake of fire and brimstone, where the beast and the false prophet are also; and they will be tormented day and night forever and ever" (Revelation 20:10).

Satan is not the problem. The problem is the fact that sinful, rebellious, prideful, and independent men and women have offended a holy God, have spurned His Son, Jesus Christ, and have sided with the enemy.

**Have you ever asked yourself, "Where are You, God? Don't You care?" Read 2 Peter 3:9. What does this passage tell you about the heart of God?**

_____

_____

_____

_____

_____

_____

_____

The final judgment is coming.

Satan is not the problem. The problem is the fact that sinful, rebellious, prideful, and independent men and women have offended a holy God, have spurned His Son, Jesus Christ, and have sided with the enemy.

If you don't know Jesus Christ, you'll be defeated. You will have no angelic assistance, because the angels have not been assigned to serve unrepentant sinners. However, the devil and his demons will make themselves at home with you, doing everything they can to keep you miserable and away from the truth.

Don't wait for Satan to oppress or possess you. Turn to the cross today, and accept Jesus Christ as your Savior, your Lord, and your God.

# NOTES

# NOTES